Learning D3.js Mapping

Build stunning maps and visualizations using D3.js

Thomas Newton

Oscar Villarreal

BIRMINGHAM - MUMBAI

Learning D3.js Mapping

First published: December 2014

Production reference: 1221214

Published by Packt Publishing Ltd.
Livery Place
35 Livery Street
Birmingham B3 2PB, UK.

ISBN 978-1-78398-560-9

www.packtpub.com

Credits

Authors

Thomas Newton

Oscar Villarreal

Reviewers

Samrat Ambadekar

Brendon Parker

Alex Rothenberg

Claudio Squarcella

Arjun Srinivasan

David Suther

Commissioning Editor

Ellen Bishop

Acquisition Editor

Rebecca Youé

Content Development Editor

Arun Nadar

Technical Editor

Pankaj Kadam

Copy Editors

Karuna Narayanan

Vikrant Phadkay

Project Coordinator

Neha Bhatnagar

Proofreaders

Simran Bhogal

Stephen Copestake

Ameesha Green

Indexer

Mariammal Chettiyar

Graphics

Abhinash Sahu

Production Coordinator

Arvindkumar Gupta

Cover Work

Arvindkumar Gupta

About the Authors

Thomas Newton has 20 years of experience in the technical industry, working on everything from low-level system designs and data visualization to software design and architecture. Currently, he is creating data visualizations to solve analytical problems for clients. When he is free, he spends as much time as possible with his family, ideally with a skateboard involved.

Oscar Villarreal has been developing interfaces for the past 10 years, and most recently, he has been focusing on data visualization and web applications. In his spare time, he loves to write on his blog, `oscarvillarreal.com`, and go rock climbing somewhere in the Rockies. He also loves to spend time with his wife and his first child.

About the Reviewers

Samrat Ambadekar is a user experience designer and prototyper, currently residing in the United States. He holds a Master's degree in Human Computer Interaction from Georgia Institute of Technology, Atlanta, and a Bachelor's degree in Computer Engineering from University of Pune, India. He has over 5 years of experience as a designer and developer, with expertise in rapid prototyping and contextual interactions. His work and interests span across UX design, interaction design, concept prototyping, 3D interactions, augmented reality, and data visualization. Apart from work, he enjoys sketching, blogging, hiking/trekking, cooking, and (occasionally) practicing kickboxing. To know more about his work, visit www.samratambadekar.com.

Alex Rothenberg has been writing software for quite a while on mobile apps, websites, and even shrink-wrapped CD-ROMs. The one constant is that he enjoys finding ways to think about complex problems in simple ways. He has really enjoyed working with D3.js recently, as visualizations are such a powerful way to convey information.

Claudio Squarcella is an InfoVis enthusiast, who possesses both theoretical and technical skills. He has a PhD in Computer Science and Engineering and is devoted to web-based network visualization. He currently works at ThousandEyes in San Francisco, where he turns network measurement data into informative graph visualization dashboards for enterprise customers.

Arjun Srinivasan is currently pursuing his graduation in computer science from the Georgia Institute of Technology, Atlanta, USA. He has a Bachelor's degree in Information Science from R. V. College of Engineering, Bangalore, India. He has worked with industry-renowned names, including SAP Labs India and Microsoft Corp. (India) along with several start-ups. His primary research interests include visual analytics, machine learning, and databases, and he focuses on how concepts from these areas can be integrated and applied in the domains of healthcare informatics and business decision-making software development. Arjun has worked with D3.js extensively for a while now, and along with using D3.js for almost all his projects, he has also developed D3.js-based plugins for two start-ups in Bangalore, India. His current projects in the visualization domain include a genome visualization project with the Georgia Aquarium and a business ecosystem visualization tool. His website can be viewed at http://arjun010.github.io/.

www.PacktPub.com

Support files, eBooks, discount offers, and more

For support files and downloads related to your book, please visit www.PacktPub.com.

Did you know that Packt offers eBook versions of every book published, with PDF and ePub files available? You can upgrade to the eBook version at www.PacktPub.com and as a print book customer, you are entitled to a discount on the eBook copy. Get in touch with us at service@packtpub.com for more details.

At www.PacktPub.com, you can also read a collection of free technical articles, sign up for a range of free newsletters and receive exclusive discounts and offers on Packt books and eBooks.

https://www2.packtpub.com/books/subscription/packtlib

Do you need instant solutions to your IT questions? PacktLib is Packt's online digital book library. Here, you can search, access, and read Packt's entire library of books.

Why subscribe?

- Fully searchable across every book published by Packt
- Copy and paste, print, and bookmark content
- On demand and accessible via a web browser

Free access for Packt account holders

If you have an account with Packt at www.PacktPub.com, you can use this to access PacktLib today and view 9 entirely free books. Simply use your login credentials for immediate access.

Table of Contents

Preface

This book explores the JavaScript library, D3.js, and its ability to help us create maps and amazing visualizations. You will no longer be confined to third-party tools in order to get a nice looking map. With D3.js, you can build your own maps and customize them as you please. This book will go from the basics of SVG and JavaScript to data trimming and modification with TopoJSON. Using D3.js to glue together these three key ingredients, we will create very attractive maps that will cover many common use cases for maps, such as choropleths, data overlays on maps, and interactivity.

What this book covers

Chapter 1, *Gather Your Cartographer's Toolbox*, covers the tools you need to install to build maps effectively with D3. We will cover the instructions to add NodeJS, npm, and TopoJSON to your system. This is needed in order to quickly bootstrap a local web server and to have the ability to manipulate map data.

Chapter 2, *Creating Images from Simple Text*, describes the basics of creating multiple shapes and designs with Scalable Vector Graphics (SVG).

Chapter 3, *Producing Graphics from Data – the Foundations of D3*, will deep dive into the main library of this book, D3.js. Concepts such as enter, update, and exit will be explained in detail with the use of some clever experiments and examples.

Chapter 4, *Creating a Map*, takes you through every step required to build a map with D3. Asynchronous loading of data, bounding box and projection creation, and TopoJSON element modification and data binding will be the bread and butter of this chapter.

Chapter 5, Click-click Boom! Applying Interactivity to Your Map, covers hover, panning, zooming, and their equivalent in touch events. Also, we'll dive into some nifty 3D projections, and *a la par*, we will learn transitions via experimentation.

Chapter 6, Finding and Working with Geographic Data, will take you through the process of acquiring data and optimizing it to your needs. This chapter covers one of the most important aspects of map visualization in detail via the use of TopoJSON.

Chapter 7, Testing, explains how to structure your codebase in order to have reusable chart components that are easily unit tested and primed for reuse in future projects.

What you need for this book

The following are the requirements for this book; these work on OS X, Windows, and Linux:

- A D3.js library v3.4.12
- NodeJS v0.10.32

Who this book is for

This book is carefully designed to allow the reader to jump between chapters based on what they are planning to get out of the book. Here is a brief guide to help you navigate the book:

- In all cases, briefly read *Chapter 1, Gather Your Cartographer's Toolbox*, as it will provide a baseline on how your system is set up to easily follow the rest of the examples.

- If you are new to SVG and D3, then read *Chapter 2, Creating Images from Simple Text*, and *Chapter 3, Producing Graphics from Data – the Foundations of D3. Chapter 3, Producing Graphics from Data – the Foundations of D3*, also provides a refresher to the enter, update, and exit pattern for those who have experience in D3.

- If you are comfortable with all these basics and ready to jump into map creation immediately, then you can proceed directly to *Chapter 4, Creating a Map*, and *Chapter 5, Click-click Boom! Applying Interactivity to Your Map*. The examples should be easy to follow and help you get bootstrapped with map making quickly.

- Once you are comfortable with map making, then *Chapter 6, Finding and Working with Geographic Data*, will help you further your craft by providing tools to help you work with the data.

- If you are interested in testing D3 visualizations (not just maps), then read *Chapter 7, Testing*. It does not assume any prior map-making knowledge and can be read independently of chapters 4, 5, and 6.

Every chapter is full of pragmatic examples that can easily provide the foundation to more complex work. We have explained, step by step, how each example works. That said, we also firmly believe in "learning by doing". As you work through the examples, continue to experiment with the sample code provided. Change the data. Change the scaling functions and colors. See how the map reacts and play with D3. Most importantly, have fun!

Conventions

In this book, you will find a number of styles of text that distinguish between different kinds of information. Here are some examples of these styles, and an explanation of their meaning.

Code words in text, database table names, folder names, filenames, file extensions, pathnames, dummy URLs, user input, and Twitter handles are shown as follows: "Then open your web browser to `http://localhost:8080`."

A block of code is set as follows:

```
<?xml version="1.0"?>
<svg width="200" height="200">
  <circle cx="60" cy="60" r="50"/>
  <circle cx ="5" cy="5" r="10" />
  <circle cx="25" cy="35" r="45" />
  <circle cx="180" cy="180" r="10"/>
  <circle cx="80" cy="130" r="40" />
  <circle cx="50" cy="50" r="5" />
  <circle cx="2" cy="2" r="7"/>
  <circle cx="77" cy="77" r="17"/>
  <circle cx="100" cy="100" r="40"/>
  <circle cx="146" cy="109" r="22"/>
</svg>
```

Any command-line input or output is written as follows:

```
npm install -g http-server
```

New terms and **important words** are shown in bold. Words that you see on the screen, in menus or dialog boxes for example, appear in the text like this: "Click on the **INSTALL** button."

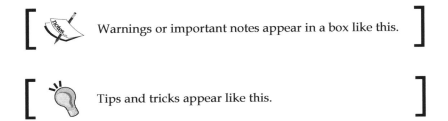

Warnings or important notes appear in a box like this.

Tips and tricks appear like this.

Reader feedback

Feedback from our readers is always welcome. Let us know what you think about this book—what you liked or disliked. Reader feedback is important for us as it helps us develop titles that you will really get the most out of.

To send us general feedback, simply e-mail feedback@packtpub.com, and mention the book's title in the subject of your message.

If there is a topic that you have expertise in and you are interested in either writing or contributing to a book, see our author guide at www.packtpub.com/authors.

Customer support

Now that you are the proud owner of a Packt book, we have a number of things to help you to get the most from your purchase.

Downloading the example code

You can download the example code files from your account at http://www.packtpub.com for all the Packt Publishing books you have purchased. If you purchased this book elsewhere, you can visit http://www.packtpub.com/support and register to have the files e-mailed directly to you.

Errata

Although we have taken every care to ensure the accuracy of our content, mistakes do happen. If you find a mistake in one of our books—maybe a mistake in the text or the code—we would be grateful if you could report this to us. By doing so, you can save other readers from frustration and help us improve subsequent versions of this book. If you find any errata, please report them by visiting `http://www.packtpub.com/submit-errata`, selecting your book, clicking on the **Errata Submission Form** link, and entering the details of your errata. Once your errata are verified, your submission will be accepted and the errata will be uploaded to our website or added to any list of existing errata under the Errata section of that title.

To view the previously submitted errata, go to `https://www.packtpub.com/books/content/support` and enter the name of the book in the search field. The required information will appear under the **Errata** section.

Piracy

Piracy of copyrighted material on the Internet is an ongoing problem across all media. At Packt, we take the protection of our copyright and licenses very seriously. If you come across any illegal copies of our works in any form on the Internet, please provide us with the location address or website name immediately so that we can pursue a remedy.

Please contact us at `copyright@packtpub.com` with a link to the suspected pirated material.

We appreciate your help in protecting our authors and our ability to bring you valuable content.

Questions

If you have a problem with any aspect of this book, you can contact us at `questions@packtpub.com`, and we will do our best to address the problem.

1
Gather Your Cartographer's Toolbox

Welcome to the world of cartography with D3. In this chapter, you will be given all the tools you need to create a map using D3. These tools exist freely and openly, thanks to the wonderful world of open source. Given that we are going to be speaking in terms of the Web, our languages will be HTML, CSS, and JavaScript. After reading this book, you will be able to use all three languages effectively in order to create maps on your own.

When creating maps in D3, your toolbox is extraordinarily light. The goal is to focus on creating data visualizations and remove the burden of heavy IDEs and map-making software. The building blocks are as follows:

- **Quick bootstrap**: We will cover installing Node.js, npm, and a lightweight server.

- **TopoJSON**: We will see the working of this tool that is used to manage and optimize geographic information.

- **Web browser as a development tool**: We will learn how to use a modern web browser, capable of rendering SVG files with built-in development tools. Some examples of common web browsers are Chrome, Firefox, Safari, and IE 9+.

 All screenshots and commands in this book have been done using Chrome. Therefore, we strongly recommend you to use this browser.

- **Installing sample code**: We will take the first steps in getting to grips with coding.

- **Working with developer tools**: We will get familiar with developer tools.

Quick bootstrap

If you're already familiar with working in D3 or web development, go ahead and set up your workstation based on the following commands by jumping directly to the *Step-by-step bootstrap* section.

A detailed explanation of this chapter's concepts will be covered if further instructions are needed. By the end of the chapter, you should feel comfortable in using the *Quick bootstrap* section as a convention throughout the book. The following instructions assume that Node.js and npm are already installed on your system.

Type in the following in the command line:

```
# Install a light webserver
npm install -g http-server


# Install topojson
npm install -g topojson


# Clone the sample code with included libraries
git clone --depth=1 git@github.com:climboid/d3jsMaps.git


# start the project
cd d3jsMaps
http-server
```

Downloading the example code

You can download the example code files from your account at `http://www.packtpub.com` for all the Packt Publishing books you have purchased. If you purchased this book elsewhere, you can visit `http://www.packtpub.com/support` and register to have the files e-mailed directly to you.

Now, open your web browser to `http://localhost:8080/chapter-1/example-1.html`, and you should see the following map:

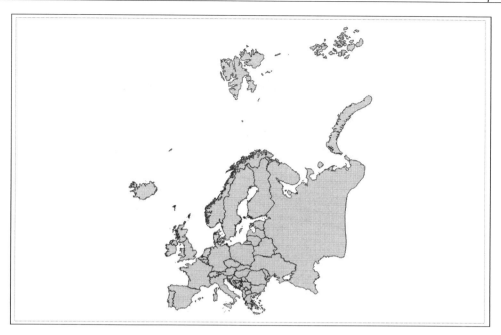

Step-by-step bootstrap

The next section covers detailed instructions to set up your development
environment to rapidly create visualizations in later chapters. By the end of the
chapter, you will have a working environment for the rest of the book (an example
of a map running and an initial look at tools used to create visualizations).

A lightweight web server

Technically, most of the content we will craft can render directly in the browser
without the use of a web server. However, we highly recommend you not to
go ahead with this approach. Running a web server in your local development
environment is extremely easy and provides several benefits:

- Geographic information, statistical data, and visualization code can be clearly
  separated into isolated files

- API calls can be stubbed and simulated, allowing easy integration into a
  full-stack application in the future

- It will prevent common mistakes when making AJAX calls to fetch
  geographic and statistical data (for example, the same-origin policy)

For our choice of the web server and other tools in our toolbox, we will rely on a Node.js package named `http-server`. Node.js is a platform built on Chrome's JavaScript runtime, which is used to build fast, scalable network applications. The platform includes **Node Package Manager (npm)**, which was created by other members of the vibrant Node.js community and allows the developer to quickly install packages of prebuilt software.

To install Node.js, simply perform the following steps:

1. Go to the website `http://nodejs.org`.
2. Click on the **INSTALL** button.
3. Open the downloaded package and follow the defaults.

To test the installation, type in the following in the command line:

```
node -v
v0.10.26 # or something similar should return
```

Now that Node.js and npm are installed, we can proceed to install the web server. When the web server is installed globally with the -g command, it becomes easily accessible throughout the system.

Once on the command line, enter the following:

```
npm install -g http-server
```

You can quickly verify the package was installed by typing the following:

```
http-server
```

Then open your web browser to `http://localhost:8080`. The browser should display a list of all the files in the directory from where you initiated the command.

Optimizing geographic data files with TopoJSON

The topojson is a command-line utility used to create files in the TopoJSON-serialized format. The TopoJSON format will be discussed in detail in *Chapter 6, Finding and Working with Geographic Data*. The topojson utility is also installed via npm.

 Note that we will use the syntax *TopoJSON* to refer to the JSON format and *topojson* to indicate the command-line utility.

We already have installed Node.JS and npm, so enter the following on the command line:

```
npm install -g topojson
```

Once the installation is complete, you should check the version of topojson installed on your machine just as we did with Node.js:

```
topojson –version
```

If you see Version 1.x, it means you have successfully installed topojson.

> topojson uses node-gyp that has several dependencies based on the operating system. Please go to `http://github.com/TooTallNate/node-gyp` for details.
>
> If you're using Windows, the basic steps are as follows:
> - Install Python 2.x (3.x not supported at the time of writing this book)
> - Install Microsoft Visual Studio C++ 2012 for Desktop (Express)

Using the web browser as a development tool

Although any modern browser supports SVG and has some kind of console, we strongly recommend you to use Google Chrome for these examples. It comes bundled with developer tools that will allow you to very easily open, explore, and modify the code. If you are not using Google Chrome, please go to `http://www.google.com/chrome` and install Google Chrome.

Installing the sample code

Go to `https://github.com/climboid/d3jsMaps` and either clone the repo, if you are familiar with Git cloning, or simply download the zipped version. Once it is downloaded, make sure to extract the file if you have it zipped.

Use the command prompt or terminal to go to the directory where you downloaded your file. For instance, if you downloaded the file to your desktop, type in the following:

```
cd ~/Desktop/d3jsMaps
http-server
```

The last command will launch the simple server we installed previously for the supplied sample code. This means that, if you open your browser and go to `http://localhost:8080/chapter-1/example-1.html`, you should see a map of Europe, similar to the one shown earlier.

Working with the developer tools

It's time to open the developer tools. On the top-right corner of the browser, you will see the icon as shown in the following screenshot:

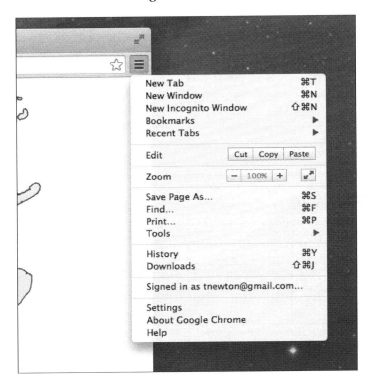

This icon opens a submenu. Click on **Tools**. Then click on **Developer tools**. A panel will open at the bottom of the browser, containing all the developer tools at your disposal.

 The option names mentioned here might differ according to the version of Chrome you are using.

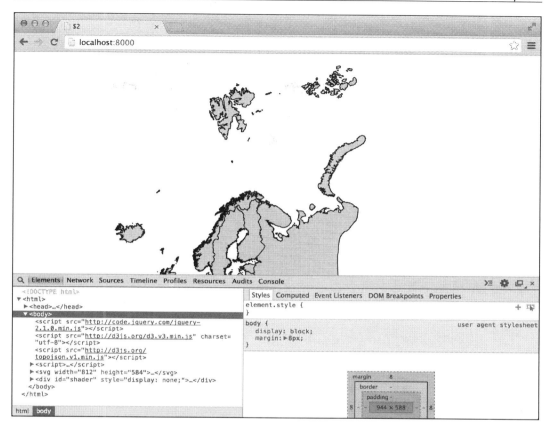

 For quick access to developer tools on the Mac, use *alt + command + I*; for Windows PCs, use *Ctrl + Shift + I*.

Within developer tools, you have a series of tabs (**Elements**, **Network**, **Sources**, and so on). These tools are extremely valuable and will allow you to inspect different aspects of your code. For more information on the Chrome developer tools, please go to the link `https://developer.chrome.com/devtools/docs/authoring-development-workflow`.

Since we are going to focus on the **Elements** tab, click on it if it is not already selected.

You should see something similar to the preceding screenshot; it will have the following code statement:

```
<svg width="812" height="584">
```

If you click on the SVG item, you should see it expand and display the path tag. The path tag will have several numbers and characters tied to a d attribute. These numbers are control points that draw the path. We will cover how the path is drawn in the next chapter and how path tags are used to create maps in *Chapter 4, Creating a Map* and *Chapter 5, Click-click Boom! Applying Interactivity to Your Map.*

We also want to draw your attention to how the HTML5 application loads the D3 library. Again in the **Elements** tag, after the SVG tag, you should see the `<script>` tag pointing to D3.js and topojson:

```
<script src="http://d3js.org/d3.v3.min.js" charset="utf-8">
</script>
<script src="http://d3js.org/topojson.v1.min.js"></script>
```

If you click on the path located inside the SVG tag, you will see a new panel called the CSS inspector or the styles inspector. It shows and controls all the styles that are applied to a selected element—in this case the path element.

These three components create a D3 visualization:

- HTML5 (the SVG and path elements)
- JavaScript (the D3.js library and map code)
- CSS (the styling of the HTML5 elements)

Creating maps and visualizations using these three components will be discussed and analyzed throughout the book.

Summary

This chapter reveals a quick glimpse of the steps for basic setup in order to have a well-organized code base to create maps with D3. You should become familiar with this setup because we will be using this convention throughout the book.

The remaining chapters will focus on creating detailed maps and achieving realistic visualizations through HTML, JavaScript, and CSS.

Let's jump right in!

2
Creating Images from Simple Text

In this chapter, a high-level overview of **Scalable Vector Graphics (SVG)** will be presented by explaining how it operates and what elements it encompasses. In a browser context, SVG is very similar to HTML and is one of the means by which D3 expresses its power. Understanding the nodes and attributes of SVG will empower us to create many kinds of visualizations, not just maps. This chapter includes the following points:

- A general SVG overview and key elements
- The SVG coordinate system
- The primary elements of SVG (lines, rectangles, circles, polygons, and paths)

Introduction – general knowledge

SVG, an XML markup language, is designed to describe two-dimensional vector graphics. The SVG markup language resides in the DOM as a node that describes exactly how to draw a shape (a curve, line, circle, and polygon). Just like HTML, SVG tags can also be styled from standard CSS. Note that, because all commands reside in the DOM, the more shapes you have, the more nodes you have and the more work for the browser. This is important to remember because, as SVG visualizations become more complex, the less fluidly they will perform.

The main SVG node is declared as follows:

```
<svg width="200" height="200"></svg>
```

This node's basic properties are width and height; they provide the primary container for the other nodes that make up a visualization. For example, if you wanted to create ten sequential circles in a 200 x 200 box, the tags would look like this:

```
<?xml version="1.0"?>
<svg width="200" height="200">
  <circle cx="60" cy="60" r="50"/>
  <circle cx ="5" cy="5" r="10"/>
  <circle cx="25" cy="35" r="45"/>
  <circle cx="180" cy="180" r="10"/>
  <circle cx="80" cy="130" r="40"/>
  <circle cx="50" cy="50" r="5"/>
  <circle cx="2" cy="2" r="7"/>
  <circle cx="77" cy="77" r="17"/>
  <circle cx="100" cy="100" r="40"/>
  <circle cx="146" cy="109" r="22"/>
</svg>
```

Note that 10 circles would need 10 nodes in the DOM, plus its container.

SVG contains several primitives that allow the developer to draw shapes quickly. We will cover the following primitives throughout this chapter:

- `circle`: A standard circle with a defined radius and position attributes
- `rect`: A standard rectangle with height, width, and position attributes
- `polygon`: Any polygon, described by a list of points
- `line`: A line with start and end points
- `path`: A complex line created through a series of drawing commands

Positioning elements

What about position? Where do these primitives draw inside the SVG element? What if you wanted to put a circle on the top left and another one on the bottom right? Where do you start?

SVG is positioned by a grid system, similar to the Cartesian coordinate system. However, in SVG (0,0) is the top-left corner. The x axis proceeds horizontally from left to right starting at 0. The y axis also starts at 0 and extends downward. See the following illustration:

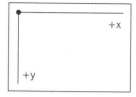

What about drawing shapes on top of each other? How do you control the z index? In SVG, there is no z coordinate. Depth is determined by the order in which the shape is drawn. If you were to draw a circle with coordinates (10,10) and then another one with coordinates (10,10), you would see the second circle drawn on top of the first.

The following sections will cover the basic SVG primitives for drawing shapes and some of their most common attributes.

Line

The SVG line is one of the simplest in the library. It draws a straight line from one point to another. The syntax is very straightforward and can be experimented with at `http://localhost:8080/chapter-2/line.html`, assuming the http-server is running:

```
<line x1="10" y1="10" x2="100" y2="100" stroke-width="1"
stroke="red"/>
```

This will give you the following output:

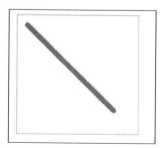

A description of the element's attributes is as follows:

- `x1` and `y1`: The starting x and y coordinates
- `x2` and `y2`: The ending x and y coordinates
- `stroke`: This gives the line a red color
- `stroke-width`: This denotes in pixels the width of the line to be drawn

The `line` tag also has the ability to change the style of the end of the line. For example, adding the following would change the image so it has round endings:

```
stroke-linecap: round;
```

As stated earlier, all SVG tags can also be styled with CSS elements. An alternative way of producing the same graphic would be to first create a CSS style, as shown in the following code:

```
line {
    stroke: red;
    stroke-linecap: round;
    stroke-width: 5;
}
```

Then you can create a very simple SVG tag using the following code:

```
<line x1="10" y1="10" x2="100" y2="100"></line>
```

More complex lines, as well as curves, can be achieved with the `path` tag; we will cover in the *Path* section.

Rectangle

The basic HTML code to create a rectangle is as follows:

```
<rect width="100" height="20" x="10" y="10"></rect>
```

Let's apply the following style:

```
rect {
    stroke-width: 1;
    stroke:steelblue;
    fill:#888;
    fill-opacity: .5;
}
```

We will create a rectangle that starts at the coordinates (10,10), and is 100 pixels wide and 20 pixels high. Based on the styling, it will have a blue outline, a gray interior, and will appear slightly opaque. See the following output and example `http://localhost:8080/chapter-2/rectangle.html`:

There are two more attributes that are useful when creating rounded borders (`rx` and `ry`):

```
<rect with="100" height="20" x="10" y="10" rx="5" ry="5"></rect>
```

These attributes indicate that the *x* and *y* corners will have 5-pixel curves.

Circle

A circle is positioned with the `cx` and `cy` attributes. These indicate the *x* and *y* coordinates of the center of the circle. The radius is determined by the `r` attribute. The following is an example you can experiment with: `http://localhost:8080/chapter-2/circle.html`:

```
<circle cx="62" cy="62" r="50"></circle>
```

Now type in the following code:

```
circle {
    stroke-width: 5;
    stroke:steelblue;
    fill:#888;
    fill-opacity: .5;
}
```

This will create a circle with the familiar blue outline, a gray interior, and half-way opaque:

Polygon

To create a polygon, use the `polygon` tag. The best way to think about an SVG polygon is to compare it to a child's dot-to-dot game. You can imagine a series of dots and a pen connecting each (x,y) coordinate with a straight line. The series of *dots* is identified in the `points` attribute. Take the following as an example (`http://localhost:8080/chapter-2/polygon.html`):

```
<polygon points="60,5 10,120 115,120"/>
```

First, we start at `60,5` and we move to `10,120`. Then, we proceed to `115,120` and finally return to `60,5` (note that the pen returns to the starting position automatically.)

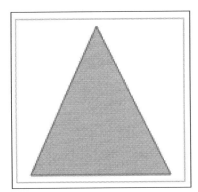

Path

When creating maps with D3, the `path` SVG tag is used most often. Using the definition from W3C, you can think of the `path` tag as a series of commands that explain how to draw any shape by moving a pen on a piece of paper. The `path` commands start with the location to place the pen on and then contain a series of follow-up commands that tell the pen how to connect additional points with lines. The path shapes can also be filled or have their outline styled.

Let's look at a very simple example to replicate the triangle we created as a polygon.

Open your browser, go to `http://localhost:8080/chapter-2/path.html`, and you will see the following output on your screen:

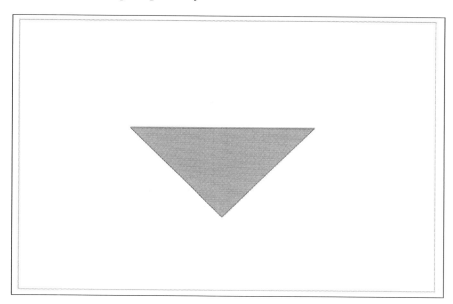

Right-click anywhere in the triangle and select **Inspect element**.

The `path` command for this shape is as follows:

```
<path d="M 120 120 L 220 220, 420 120 Z" stroke="steelblue"
fill="lightyellow" stroke-width="2"></path>
```

The attribute that contains the path drawing commands is d. The commands adhere to the following structure:

- M: Put the pen down to start drawing at x = 120 y = 120
- L: Draw a straight line that connects (120,120) to x = 220 y = 220, then draw another straight line that connects (220,220) to x = 420 y = 120
- Z: Connect the last data point (420,120) to where we started (120,120)

Experiment

Let's try some experiments to reinforce what we just learned. From the Chrome developer tools, simply remove the z at the end of the path and hit enter:

```
▼<svg height="300" width="450">
    <path d="M 120 120 L 220 220, 320 120 Z"></path>
</svg>
```

You should see the top line disappear. Try some other experiments with changing the data points in the L subcommand.

Paths with curves

Paths can also have curves. The concept is still the same; you connect several data points with lines. The main difference is that now you apply a curve to each line as it connects the dots. There are three types of curve commands:

- Cubic Bézier
- Quadratic Bézier
- Elliptical Arc

Each command is explained in detail at http://www.w3.org/TR/SVG11/paths.html. As an example, let's apply a cubic Bézier curve to the triangle. The format for the command is as follows:

```
C x1 y1 x2 y2 x y
```

This command can be inserted into the path structure at any point:

- C: Indicates that we are applying a Cubic Bézier curve, just as L in the previous example indicates a straight line
- x1 and y1: Adds a control point to influence the curve's tangent
- x2 and y2: Adds a second control point after applying x1 and y1
- x and y: Indicates the final resting place of the line

To apply this command to our previous triangle, we need to replace the second line command (320 120) with a cubic command (C 200 70 480 290 320 120).

Before the statement was:

```
<path d="M 120 120 L 220 220, 320 120 Z"></path>
```

After adding cubic command it will be:

```
<path d="M 120 120 L 220 220, C 200 70 480 290 320 120 Z"></path>
```

This will produce the following shape:

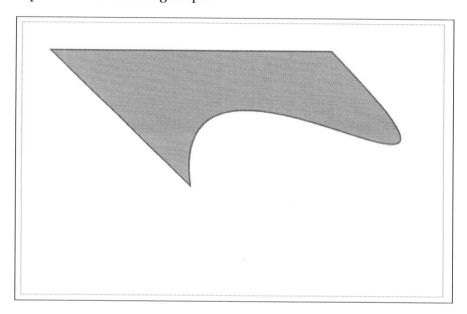

To illustrate how the cubic Bézier curve works, let's draw circles and lines to show the control points in the C command:

```
<svg  height="300" width="525">
    <path d="M 120 120 L 220 220 C 200 70 480 290 320 120 Z ">
    </path>
    <line x1="220"  y1="220" x2="200" y2="70"></line>
    <circle cx="200" cy="70" r="5" ></circle>
    <line x1="200"  y1="70"  x2="480" y2="290"></line>
    <circle cx="480" cy="290"  r="5"></circle>
    <line x1="480"  y1="290" x2="320" y2="120"></line>
</svg>
```

The output should look like the one shown in the following screenshot and can be experimented with at `http://localhost:8080/chapter-2/curves.html`. You can see the angles created by the control points (indicated by circles in the output) and the cubic Bézier curves applied.

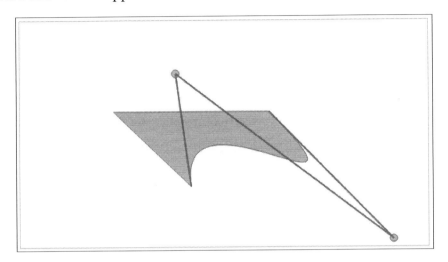

SVG paths are the main tool leveraged when drawing geographic regions. However, imagine if you were to draw an entire map by hand using SVG paths; the task would become exhausting! For example, the command structure for the map of Europe in our first chapter has 3,366,121 characters in it! Even a simple state such as Colorado would be a lot of code if executed by hand:

```
<path xmlns="http://www.w3.org/2000/svg" id="CO_1_"
style="fill:#ff0000" d="M 115.25800,104.81000 L
116.51200,84.744000 L 117.00000,77.915000 L 106.82700,77.077000 L
99.371000,76.452000 L 88.014000,75.198000 L 81.709000,74.431000 L
80.907000,81.189000 L 79.932000,88.018000 L 78.788000,96.547000 L
78.329000,99.932000 L 78.154000,101.11800 L 88.641000,102.37200 L
99.898000,103.72200 L 109.88400,104.39200 L 111.91300,104.60300 L
115.39700,104.77700"/>
```

We will learn in later chapters how D3 will come to the rescue.

Transform

Transform allows you to change your visualization dynamically and is one of the advantages of using SVG and commands to draw shapes. Transform is an additional attribute you can add to any of the elements we have discussed so far. Two important types of transforms when dealing with our D3 maps are:

- **Translate**: Move the element
- **Scale**: Adjust the coordinates for all attributes in the element

Translate

You will likely use this transformation in all of your cartography work and will see it in most D3 examples online. As a technique, it's often used with a margin object to shift the entire visualization. The following syntax can be applied to any element:

```
transform="translate(x,y)"
```

Here, *x* and *y* are the coordinates to move the element by.

For example, a translate transform can move our circle 50 pixels to the left and 50 pixels down by using the following code:

```
<circle cx="62" cy="62" r="50" transform="translate(50,50)"></circle>
```

Here is the output:

Note that the translucent image represents the original image and the location the shape moved from. The `translate` attribute is not an absolute position. It adjusts the origin of the circle relatively to `cx`, `cy` and adds 50 to those coordinates. If you were to move the circle to the top left of the container, you would translate with negative values. For example:

```
transform="translate(-10,-10)"
```

Feel free to experiment in your Chrome developer tools or code editor at `http://localhost:8080/chapter-2/translate.html`.

Scale

The scale transform is easy to understand but often creates undesired effects if you lose the focus of where the scaling originated.

Scale adjusts the (x,y) values across all attributes in the element. Using the earlier `circle` code, we have the following:

```
<circle cx="62" cy="62" r="50" stroke-width="5" fill="red"
transform="scale(2,2)"></circle>
```

The scale is going to double the `cx`, `cy`, radius, and `stroke-width`, producing the following output (`http://localhost:8080/chapter-2/scale.html`):

It is important to emphasize that, because we are using SVG commands to draw the shapes, there is no loss of quality as we scale the images, unlike raster images such as PNG or JPEG. The transform types can be combined to adjust for scale, altering the *x* and *y* position of the shape. Let's use the path example that we used earlier in the following code:

```
<path d="M 120 120 L 220 220 C 200 70 480 290 320 120 Z"
stroke="steelblue" fill="lightyellow" stroke-width="2"
transform="translate(-200,-200), scale(2,2)"></path>
```

The preceding code will produce the following output (`http://localhost:8080/chapter-2/scale_translate.html`):

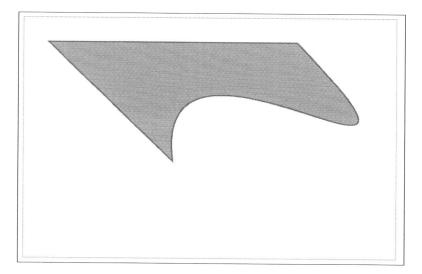

Grouping

The group tag `<g>` is used often in SVG, especially in maps. It is used to group elements and then apply a set of attributes to that set. It provides the following benefits:

- It allows you to treat a set of shapes as a single shape for the purpose of scaling and translating.

- It prevents code duplication by allowing you to set attributes at a higher level and have them inherit to all the elements included.

- Groups are essential for applying transformations to large sets of SVG nodes in a performant manner. Grouping offsets the parent group rather than modifying each of the attributes in every item of the group.

Let's take the set of shapes used to explain Bézier curves and add all of them to a single group, combining everything we have learned so far, in the following code:

```
<svg height="500" width="800">
  <g transform="translate(-200,-100), scale(2,2)">
    <path d="M 120 120 L 220 220 C 200 70 480 290 320 120 Z">
    </path>

    <line x1="220"  y1="220" x2="200" y2="70"></line>
    <circle cx="200" cy="70"   r="5" ></circle>

    <line x1="200"  y1="70"   x2="480" y2="290"></line>
    <circle cx="480" cy="290"  r="5" ></circle>

    <line x1="480"  y1="290" x2="320" y2="120"></line>
  </g>
</svg>
```

The preceding code will produce the following image (`http://localhost:8080/chapter-2/group.html`):

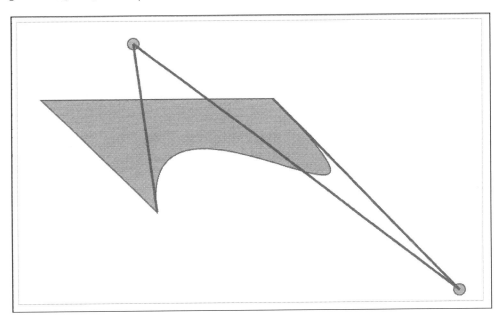

Without using the group element, we would have had to apply transform, translate, and scale to all six shapes in the set. Grouping helps us save time and allows us to make quick alignment tweaks in the future.

Text

The text element, as its name describes, is used to display text in SVG. The basic HTML code to create a text node is as follows:

```
<text x="250" y="150">Hello world!</text>
```

It has an *x* and a *y* coordinate to tell it where to begin writing in the SVG coordinate system. Styling can be achieved with a CSS class in order to have a clear separation of concerns within our code base. For example, check out the following code:

```
<text x="250" y="150" class="myText">Hello world!</text>

.myText{
  font-size:22px;
  font-family:Helvetica;
  stroke-width:2;
}
```

Text also supports rotation in order to provide flexibility when positioning it on the visualization:

```
<svg width="600" height="600">
        <text x="250" y="150" class="myText"
        transform="rotate(45,200,0)" font-family="Verdana"
        font-size="100">Hello world!</text>
</svg>
```

Some examples are located at `http://localhost:8080/chapter-2/text.html` and displayed as shown in the following image:

Keep in mind that, if you rotate the text, it will rotate relative to its origin (x and y). You can specify the origin of the translation via `cx` and `cy` or in this case `250,150`. See the `transform` property in the code for more clarity.

Summary

This chapter has given us a wealth of SVG information. We explained paths, lines, circles, rectangles, text, and some of their attributes. We also covered transformation by scaling and translating shapes. Since this chapter has given us a solid baseline, we can now create complicated shapes. The next chapter will introduce us to D3 and how it is used to manage SVG programmatically. On we go!

3
Producing Graphics from Data – the Foundations of D3

We have acquired our toolbox and reviewed the basics of SVG. It is now time to explore D3.js. D3 is the evolution of the Protovis (`http://mbostock.github.io/protovis/`) library. If you delved into data visualization or were interested in making charts for your web application, you might have used this library. Additional libraries existed that could be differentiated by how fast they rendered graphics and their compatibility with different browsers. For example, Internet Explorer did not support SVG but used its own implementation, VML. This made the Raphaël library an excellent option because Raphaël automatically mapped to either VML or SVG. On the other hand, the easiness of jqPlot and its simplistic jQuery plugin interface allowed developers to adopt it very quickly.

However, Protovis had something different. Given the vector nature of the library, it allowed you to illustrate different kinds of visualizations, as well as generate fluid transitions. Please feel free to look at the links provided and see for yourself. Examine the force-directed layout at `http://mbostock.github.io/protovis/ex/force.html`. In 2010, these were interesting and compelling visualizations, especially for the browser.

Inspired by Protovis, a team at Stanford University consisting of Jeff Heer, Mike Bostock, and Vadim Ogievetsky began to focus on D3. D3 and its application to SVG gave developers an easy way to bind their visualizations to data and add interactivity.

There is a wealth of information available to research D3. A great resource for complete coverage can be found on the D3 website at `https://github.com/mbostock/d3/wiki`. In this chapter, we will introduce the following concepts that will be used throughout this book:

- Creating basic SVG elements
- Enter
- Update
- Exit
- AJAX

Creating basic SVG elements

A common operation in D3 is to select a DOM element and append SVG elements. Subsequent calls will then set the SVG attributes, which we learned about in *Chapter 2, Creating Images from Simple Text*. D3 accomplishes this operation through an easy-to-read functional syntax called method chaining. Let's walk through a very simple example to illustrate how this is accomplished (go to `http://localhost:8080/chapter-3/example-1.html` if you have the http-server running):

```
var svg = d3.select("body")
    .append("svg")
    .attr("width", 200)
    .attr("height", 200)
```

First, we select the `body` tag and append an SVG element to it. This SVG element has a width and height of 200 pixels. We also store the selection in a variable:

```
svg.append('rect')
    .attr('x', 10)
    .attr('y', 10)
    .attr("width",50)
    .attr("height",100);
```

Next, we use the `svg` variable and append a `<rect>` item to it. This `rect` item will start at (10,10) and will have a width of 50 and a height of 100. From your Chrome browser, open the Chrome developer tools with the **Elements** tab selected and inspect the SVG element.

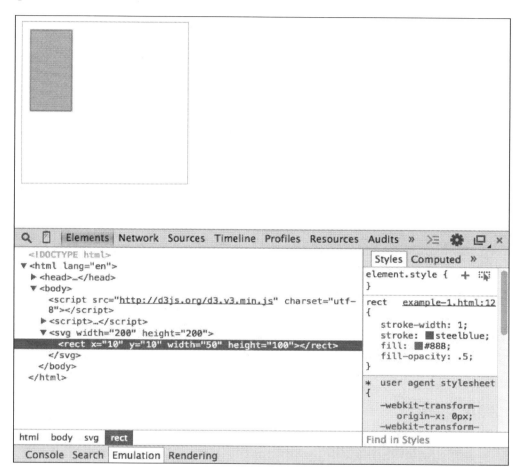

Notice the pattern: `append('svg')` creates `<svg></svg>` and `attr('width',200)` as well as `attr('height',200)` set `width="200"` and `height="200"`. Together, they produce the SVG syntax we learned about in the previous chapter:

```
<svg width="200" height="200">...</svg>
```

Enter

The enter function is a part of every basic D3 visualization. It allows the developer to define a starting point with attached data. The enter function can be thought of as a section of code that executes when data is applied to the visualization for the first time. Typically, the enter section will follow the selection of a DOM element. Let's walk through an example (http://localhost:8080/chapter-3/example-2.html):

```
var svg = d3.select("body")
    .append("svg")
    .attr("width", 200)
    .attr("height", 200);
```

Create the SVG container as we did earlier:

```
svg.selectAll('rect').data([1,2]).enter()
```

The data function is the way we bind data to our selection. In this example, we are binding a very simple array, [1,2], to the selection <rect>. The enter function will loop through the [1,2] array and apply the subsequent function calls, as shown in the following code:

```
.append('rect')
.attr('x', function(d){ return d*20; })
.attr('y', function(d){ return d*50; })
```

As we loop through each element in the array, we will:

- Append a new rect SVG element
- Position the rect element in coordinate $x = d * 20$ and $y = d * 50$ for the element, where d is equal to 1 for the first element and 2 for the second element

```
.attr("width",50)
.attr("height",100);
```

We will keep the height and width the same.

```
<svg width="200" height="200">
  <rect x="20" y="50" width="50" height="100"></rect>
  <rect x="40" y="100" width="50" height="100"></rect>
</svg>
```

Look closely; take a peek at the Chrome developer tools. We see two rectangles, each corresponding to one element in our array!

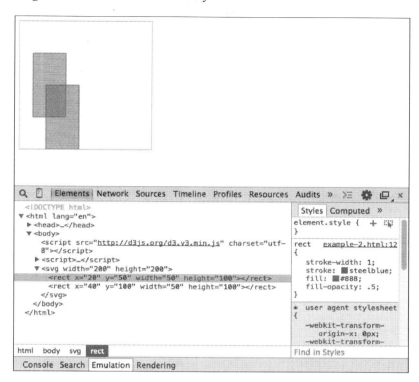

Remember that data doesn't necessarily have to be boring, such as the numbers 1 or 2. It can be any data object. To illustrate this, we will change the previous array to an array of objects in the next example (see example `http://localhost:8080/chapter-3/example-3.html`):

```
var data = [
  {
    x:10,
    y:10,
    width:5,
    height:40
  },{
    x:40,
    y:10,
    width:100,
    height:40
  }
```

```
];

    var svg = d3.select("body")
      .append("svg")
      .attr("width", 200)
      .attr("height", 200);

    svg.selectAll('rect').data(data).enter()
      .append('rect')
      .attr('x', function(d){ return d.x})
      .attr('y', function(d){ return d.y})
      .attr("width", function(d){ return d.width})
      .attr("height", function(d){ return d.height});
```

Now, as we loop through each object in the array, we will:

- Still append a new `rect` SVG element.
- Position and size the `rect` element by the properties of the object. The first rectangle will be positioned at x=10, y=10, and have a width of 5 and a height of 40. The second rectangle will be positioned at 40, 10, and will have a width of 100 and a height of 40.

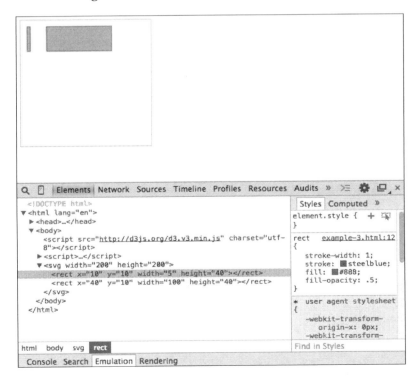

Update

Not only do we have our rectangles but we've also joined them to a dataset composed of two objects. Both objects share the same properties, namely x, y, width, and height, so it's easy to loop through them and read/bind the values to our visualization. The output of this is a set of static SVG elements. This section will cover how to update the SVG elements and properties as the joined data changes. Let's enhance the previous example to explain exactly how this works (`http://localhost:8080/chapter-3/example-4.html`):

```
function makeData(n){
  var arr = [];

  for (var i=0; i<n; i++){
    arr.push({
      x:Math.floor((Math.random() * 100) + 1),
      y:Math.floor((Math.random() * 100) + 1),
      width:Math.floor((Math.random() * 100) + 1),
      height:Math.floor((Math.random() * 100) + 1)
    })
  };

  return arr;
}
```

This function creates a new array of objects with random properties for x, y, width, and height. We can use this to simulate a change in data, allowing us to create *n* number of items, all with different properties:

```
var rectangles = function(svg) {
```

Here, we create a function that inserts rectangles into the DOM on every invocation with D3. The description is as follows:

```
var data = makeData(2);
```

Let's generate our fake data:

```
var rect = svg.selectAll('rect').data(data);
```

Let's select our rectangle and assign our data to it. This gives us a variable to which we can easily apply `enter` and `update` later. The following sections are written in a verbose way to illustrate exactly what is going on with `enter`, `update`, and `exit`. While it's possible to take shortcuts in D3, it's best to stick to this style to prevent confusion:

```
// Enter
rect.enter().append('rect')
  .attr('test', function(d,i) {
    // Enter called 2 times only
    console.log('enter placing initial rectangle: ', i)
  });
```

As in the previous section, for each element in the array we append a rectangle tag to the DOM. If you're running this code in your Chrome browser, you will notice that the console only displays `enter placing initial rectangle` twice. This is because the `enter()` section is called only when there are more elements in the array than in the DOM:

```
// Update
rect.transition().duration(500).attr('x', function(d){
  return d.x; })
    .attr('y', function(d){ return d.y; })
    .attr('width', function(d){ return d.width; })
    .attr('height', function(d){ return d.height; })
    .attr('test', function(d, i) {
      // update every data change
      console.log('updating x position to: ', d.x)
    });
```

The update section is executed for every element in the data array. In the previous example, we set the x, y, width, and height attributes of the rectangle for every data object. The update section is not defined with an explicit `update` method. D3 implies an update call if no other section is provided. If you are running the code in your Chrome browser, you will see the console display `updating x position to:` every time the data changes:

```
var svg = d3.select("body")
    .append("svg")
    .attr("width", 200)
    .attr("height", 200);
```

The following command inserts our working SVG container:

```
rectangles(svg);
```

The following command draws the first version of our visualization:

```
setInterval(function(){
  rectangles(svg);
},1000);
```

The `setInterval` function is the JavaScript function used to execute an operation every *x* milliseconds. In this case, we are calling the `rectangles` function every 1000 milliseconds.

The `rectangles` function generates a new dataset every time it is called. It has the same property structure that we had before, but the values tied to those properties are random numbers between 1 and 100. On the first call, the enter section is invoked and we create our initial two rectangles. Every 1000 milliseconds, we reinvoke the `rectangles` function with the same data structure but different random property attributes. Because the structure is the same, the enter section is now skipped and only `update` is reapplied to the existing rectangles. This is why we get the same rectangles with different dimensions every time we plot.

Update is a very useful method. For instance, your dataset could be tied to the stock market and you would want to update your visualization every *n* milliseconds to reflect the changes in the stock market. You could also bind the update to an event triggered by a user and have the user control the visualization. The options are endless.

Exit

We've discussed `enter` and `update`. We've seen how one determines the starting point of our visualization and the other modifies its attributes based on new data coming in. However, the examples covered had the exact number of data elements with the same properties. What would happen if our new dataset had a different amount of items? What if it has fewer or more?

Let's take the `update` part of the previous example and modify it a bit to demonstrate what we're talking about (`http://localhost:8080/chapter-3/example-5.html`). We can explain how this works with two small changes to the rectangles function:

```
var rectangles = function(svg) {
  var data = makeData((Math.random() * 5) + 1);
```

Here, we tell the `data` function to create a random number of data objects:

```
var rect = svg.selectAll('rect').data(data);

// Enter
rect.enter().append('rect')
  .attr('test', function(d,i) {
    // Enter called 2 times only
    console.log('enter placing initial rectangle: ', i)
});

// Update
rect.transition().attr('x', function(d){ return d.x; })
    .attr('y', function(d){ return d.y; })
    .attr('width', function(d){ return d.width; })
    .attr('height', function(d){ return d.height; })
    .attr('test', function(d, i) {
      // update every data change
      console.log('updating x position to: ', d.x)
    });
```

The `exit` function would be the same as before. Add a new `exit()` section:

```
// Exit
rect.exit().attr('test', function(d) {
  console.log('no data...')
}).remove();
}
```

Exit serves the purpose of cleansing or cleaning the no-longer-used DOM items in our visualization. This is helpful because it allows us to join our data with DOM elements, keeping them in sync. An easy way to remember this is as follows: if there are more data elements than DOM elements, the `enter()` section will be invoked. If there are fewer data elements than DOM elements, the `exit()` section will be invoked. In the previous example, we just removed the DOM element if there is no matching data.

The following is a graphical representation of the sequence that occurs when `enter` and `update` are called. Notice that there's no DOM element for data element 6, so the enter section is executed. For data elements 0 to 5, the update code is always called. For data element 6, the update section will be executed after the enter process has completed.

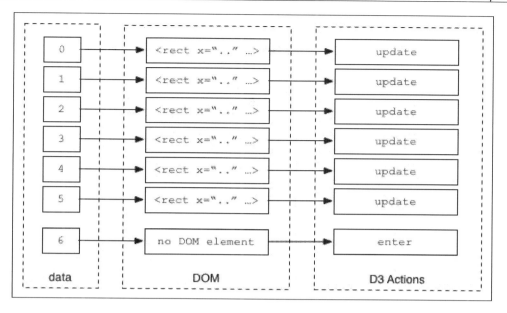

This illustrates what happens when you have fewer data elements than DOM elements. The update section is always called where there is a match, as shown in the following diagram.

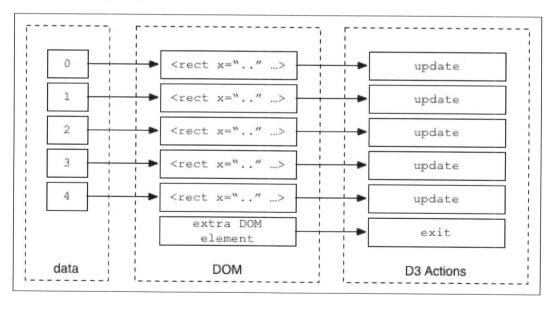

AJAX

AJAX (Asynchronous JavaScript and XML) doesn't relate 100 percent to D3. It actually has its foundation in JavaScript. In short, AJAX allows the developer to obtain data from the background of the web page. This technique is extremely useful in map development because geographic datasets can be very large. Acquiring the data from the background will help produce a refined user experience. In addition, in *Chapter 6, Finding and Working with Geographic Data*, we will cover techniques to compress the size of geographic data.

Separating the data from the code base will also provide the following advantages:

- A lighter code base that is easier to manage
- The ability to update the data without making code changes
- The ability to use third-party providers for data sources

This is accomplished by acquiring the data through an AJAX call with the aid of a D3 function. Let's examine the following code:

```
d3.json("data/dataFile.json", function(error, json) {
```

The `d3.json` method has two parameters: a path to the file and a callback function. The callback function indicates what to do with the data once it has been transferred. In the previous code, if the call fetches the data correctly, it assigns it to the `json` variable. The `error` variable is just a general error object that indicates whether there were any problems fetching the data or not:

```
if (error) return console.log(error);
var data = json;
```

We store our JSON data into the data variable and continue to process it as we did in the previous examples:

```
    var svg = d3.select("body")
      .append("svg")
      .attr("width", 200)
      .attr("height", 200);

    svg.selectAll('rect')
      .data(data).enter()
      .append('rect')
      .attr('x', function(d){ return d.x; })
      .attr('y', function(d){ return d.y; })
      .attr("width", function(d){ return d.width; })
      .attr("height", function(d){ return d.height; });
});
```

D3 provides us with many kinds of data acquisition methods. JSON is one type and it also supports CSV files, plain text files, XML files, or even entire HTML pages. We strongly suggest that you read about AJAX in the documentation at `https://github.com/mbostock/d3/wiki/Requests`.

Summary

In this chapter, we explained the core elements of D3 (`enter`, `update`, and `exit`). We understood the power of joining data to our visualization. Not only can data come from many different sources, but it is possible to have the visualization automatically updated as well.

Many detailed examples can be found in the D3 Gallery at `https://github.com/mbostock/d3/wiki/Gallery`.

In the next chapter, we will combine all of these techniques to build our first map from scratch. Get ready!

4
Creating a Map

It's been quite a ride so far. We've gone through all the different aspects that encompass the creation of a map. We've touched on the basics of SVG, JavaScript, and D3. Now, it's time to put all the pieces together and actually have a final deliverable product. In this chapter, we will cover the following topics through a series of experiments:

- Foundation – creating your basic map
- Experiment 1 – adjusting the bounding box
- Experiment 2 – creating choropleths
- Experiment 3 – adding click events to our visualization
- Experiment 4 – using updates and transitions to enhance our visualization
- Experiment 5 – adding points of interest
- Experiment 6 – adding visualizations as a point of interest

Foundation – creating your basic map

In this section, we will walk through the basics of creating a standard map. The example can be viewed by opening the `example-1.html` file of this chapter provided with this book. If you already have the http-server running, you can point your browser to `http://localhost:8080/chapter-4/example-1.html`. On the screen is Mexico (Oscar's beloved country)!

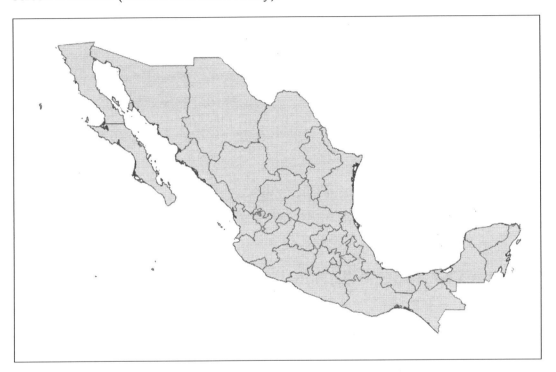

Let's walk through the code to get a step-by-step explanation of how to create this map.

The width and height can be anything you want. Depending on where your map will be visualized (cellphones, tablets, or desktops), you might want to consider providing a different width and height:

```
var height = 600;
var width = 900;
```

The next variable defines a projection algorithm that allows you to go from a cartographic space (latitude and longitude) to a Cartesian space (x,y)—basically a mapping of latitude and longitude to coordinates. You can think of a projection as a way to map the three-dimensional globe to a flat plane. There are many kinds of projections, but geo.mercator is normally the default value you will use:

```
var projection = d3.geo.mercator();
var mexico = void 0;
```

If you were making a map of the USA, you could use a better projection called albersUsa. This is to better position Alaska and Hawaii. By creating a geo.mercator projection, Alaska would render proportionate to its size, rivaling that of the entire US. The albersUsa projection grabs Alaska, makes it smaller, and puts it at the bottom of the visualization. The following screenshot is of geo.mercator:

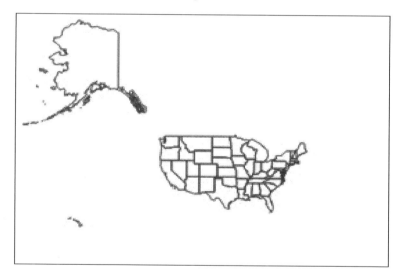

This following screenshot is of `geo.albersUsa`:

The D3 library currently contains nine built-in projection algorithms. An overview of each one can be viewed at `https://github.com/mbostock/d3/wiki/Geo-Projections`.

Next, we will assign the projection to our `geo.path` function. This is a special D3 function that will map the JSON-formatted geographic data into SVG paths. The data format that the `geo.path` function requires is named GeoJSON and will be covered in *Chapter 6, Finding and Working with Geographic Data*:

```
var path = d3.geo.path().projection(projection);
var svg = d3.select("#map")
    .append("svg")
    .attr("width", width)
    .attr("height", height);
```

Including the dataset

The necessary data has been provided for you within the data folder with the
filename geo-data.json:

```
d3.json('geo-data.json', function(data) {
    console.log('mexico', data);
```

We get the data from an AJAX call, as we saw in the previous chapter.

After the data has been collected, we want to draw only those parts of the data that
we are interested in. In addition, we want to automatically scale the map to fit the
defined height and width of our visualization.

If you look at the console, you'll see that "mexico" has an objects property. Nested
inside the objects property is MEX_adm1. This stands for the administrative areas
of Mexico. It is important to understand the geographic data you are using, because
other data sources might have different names for the administrative areas property:

```
▼ Object {type: "Topology", objects: Object, arcs: Array[934], transform: Object} 🔲
  ▶ arcs: Array[934]
  ▼ objects: Object
    ▼ MEX_adm1: Object
      ▶ bbox: Array[4]
      ▶ geometries: Array[32]
        type: "GeometryCollection"
      ▶ __proto__: Object
    ▶ __proto__: Object
  ▶ transform: Object
    type: "Topology"
  ▶ __proto__: Object
```

Notice that the MEX_adm1 property contains a geometries array with 32 elements.
Each of these elements represents a state in Mexico. Use this data to draw the
D3 visualization.

```
var states = topojson.feature(data, data.objects.MEX_adm1);
```

Here, we pass all of the administrative areas to the topojson.feature function
in order to extract and create an array of GeoJSON objects. The preceding states
variable now contains the features property. This features array is a list of
32 GeoJSON elements, each representing the geographic boundaries of a state
in Mexico. We will set an initial scale and translation to 1 and 0,0 respectively:

```
// Setup the scale and translate
projection.scale(1).translate([0, 0]);
```

This algorithm is quite useful. The bounding box is a spherical box that returns a two-dimensional array of min/max coordinates, inclusive of the geographic data passed:

```
var b = path.bounds(states);
```

To quote the D3 documentation:

> *"The bounding box is represented by a two-dimensional array: [[left, bottom], [right, top]], where left is the minimum longitude, bottom is the minimum latitude, right is maximum longitude, and top is the maximum latitude."*

This is very helpful if you want to programmatically set the scale and translation of the map. In this case, we want the entire country to fit in our height and width, so we determine the bounding box of every state in the country of Mexico.

The scale is calculated by taking the longest geographic edge of our bounding box and dividing it by the number of pixels of this edge in the visualization:

```
var s = .95 / Math.max((b[1][0] - b[0][0]) / width, (b[1][1] -
b[0][1]) / height);
```

This can be calculated by first computing the scale of the width, then the scale of the height, and, finally, taking the larger of the two. All of the logic is compressed into the single line given earlier. The three steps are explained in the following image:

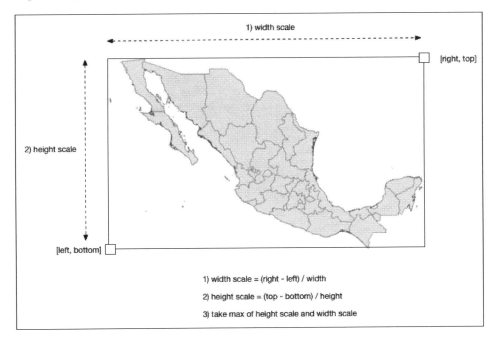

The value `95` adjusts the scale, because we are giving the map a bit of a breather on the edges in order to not have the paths intersect the edges of the SVG container item, basically reducing the scale by 5 percent.

Now, we have an accurate scale of our map, given our set width and height.

```
var t = [(width - s * (b[1][0] + b[0][0])) / 2, (height - s *
(b[1][1] + b[0][1])) / 2];
```

As we saw in *Chapter 2, Creating Images from Simple Text*, when we scale in SVG, it scales all the attributes (even x and y). In order to return the map to the center of the screen, we will use the `translate` function.

The `translate` function receives an array with two parameters: the amount to translate in x, and the amount to translate in y. We will calculate x by finding the center *(topRight – topLeft)/2* and multiplying it by the scale. The result is then subtracted from the width of the SVG element.

Our y translation is calculated similarly but using the *bottomRight – bottomLeft* values divided by 2, multiplied by the scale, then subtracted from the height.

Finally, we will reset the projection to use our new scale and translation:

```
projection.scale(s).translate(t);
```

Here, we will create a map variable that will group all of the following SVG elements into a `<g>` SVG tag. This will allow us to apply styles and better contain all of the proceeding paths' elements:

```
var map = svg.append('g').attr('class', 'boundary');
```

Finally, we are back to the classic D3 enter, update, and exit pattern. We have our data, the list of Mexico states, and we will join this data to the path SVG element:

```
mexico = map.selectAll('path').data(states.features);

//Enter
mexico.enter()
    .append('path')
    .attr('d', path);
```

The enter section and the corresponding `path` functions are executed on every data element in the array. As a refresher, each element in the array represents a state in Mexico. The `path` function has been set up to correctly draw the outline of each state as well as scale and translate it to fit in our SVG container.

Congratulations! You have created your first map!

Experiment 1 – adjusting the bounding box

Now that we have our foundation, let's start with our first experiment. For this experiment, we will manually zoom in to a state of Mexico using what we learned in the previous section. The code can be found in `example-2.html` (`http://localhost:8080/chapter-4/example-2.html`); however, feel free to edit `example-1.html` to learn as you go.

For this experiment, we will modify one line of code:

```
var b = path.bounds(states.features[5]);
```

Here, we are telling the calculation to create a boundary based on the sixth element of the features array instead of every state in the country of Mexico. The boundaries data will now run through the rest of the scaling and translation algorithms to adjust the map to the one shown in the following screenshot:

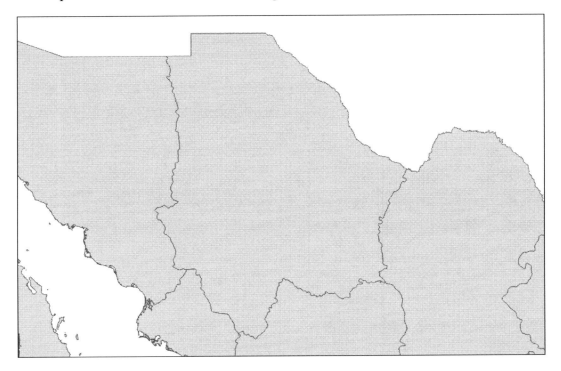

We have basically reduced the min/max of the boundary box to include the geographic coordinates for one state in Mexico (see the next screenshot), and D3 has scaled and translated this information for us automatically:

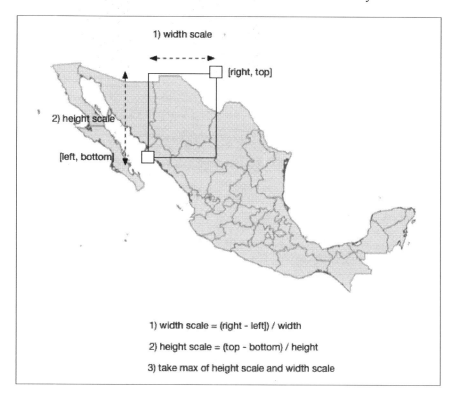

This can be very useful in situations where you might not have the data that you need in isolation from the surrounding areas. Hence, you can always zoom in to your geography of interest and isolate it from the rest.

Experiment 2 – creating choropleths

One of the most common uses of D3.js maps is to make choropleths. This visualization gives you the ability to discern between regions, giving them a different color. Normally, this color is associated with some other value, for instance, levels of influenza or a company's sales. Choropleths are very easy to make in D3.js. In this experiment, we will create a quick choropleth based on the index value of the state in the array of all the states. Look at the following code or open up your browser to `http://localhost:8080/chapter-4/example-3.html`.

We will only need to modify two lines of code in the update section of our D3 code. Right after the enter section, add the following two lines:

```
//Update
var color = d3.scale.linear().domain([0,33]).range(['red',
'yellow']);
mexico.attr('fill', function(d,i) {return color(i)});
```

The `color` variable uses another valuable D3 function named `scale`. Scales are extremely powerful when creating visualizations in D3; much more detail on scales can be found at https://github.com/mbostock/d3/wiki/Scales.

For now, let's describe what this scale defines. Here, we created a new function called `color`. This `color` function looks for any number between 0 and 33 in an input domain. D3 linearly maps these input values to a color between red and yellow in the output range. D3 has included the capability to automatically map colors in a linear range to a gradient. This means that executing the new function, `color`, with `0` will return the color red, `color(15)` will return an orange color, and `color(33)` will return yellow.

Now, in the update section, we will set the `fill` property of the path to the new color function. This will provide a linear scale of colors and use the index value `i` to determine what color should be returned.

If the color was determined by a different value of the datum, for instance, `d.sales`, then you would have a choropleth where the colors actually represent sales. The preceding code should render something as follows:

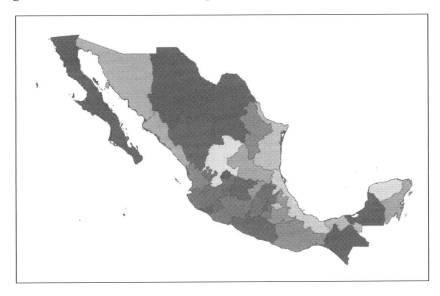

Experiment 3 – adding click events to our visualization

We've seen how to make a map and set different colors to the different regions of this map. Next, we will add a little bit of interactivity. This will illustrate a simple reference to bind click events to maps. For this experiment, we will build on the previous exercise, example-3.html. You can see the completed experiment at http://localhost:8080/chapter-4/example-4.html.

First, we need a quick reference to each state in the country. To accomplish this, we will create a new function called geoID right below the mexico variable:

```
var height = 600;
var width = 900;
var projection = d3.geo.mercator();
var mexico = void 0;

var geoID = function(d) {
  return "c" + d.properties.ID_1;
};
```

This function takes in a state data element and generates a new selectable ID based on the ID_1 property found in the data. The ID_1 property contains a unique numeric value for every state in the array. If we insert this as an id attribute into the DOM, then we would create a quick and easy way to select each state in the country.

The following is the geoID function, creating another function called click:

```
var click = function(d) {
  mexico.attr('fill-opacity', 0.2); // Another update!
  d3.select('#' + geoID(d)).attr('fill-opacity', 1);
};
```

This method makes it easy to separate what the click is doing. The click method receives the datum and changes the fill opacity value of all the states to 0.2. This is done so that when you click on one state and then on the other, the previous state does not maintain the *clicked* style. Notice that the function call is iterating through all the elements of the DOM, using the D3 update pattern. After making all the states transparent, we will set a fill-opacity of 1 for the given clicked item. This removes all the transparent styling from the selected state. Notice that we are reusing the geoID function that we created earlier to quickly find the state element in the DOM.

Next, let's update the `enter` method to bind our new `click` method to every new DOM element that `enter` appends:

```
//Enter
mexico.enter()
    .append('path')
    .attr('d', path)
    .attr('id', geoID)
    .on("click", click);
```

We also added an attribute called `id`; this inserts the results of the `geoID` function into the `id` attribute. Again, this makes it very easy to find the clicked state.

The code base should produce a map as follows. Check it out and make sure that you click on any of the states. You will see its color turn a little brighter than the surrounding states.

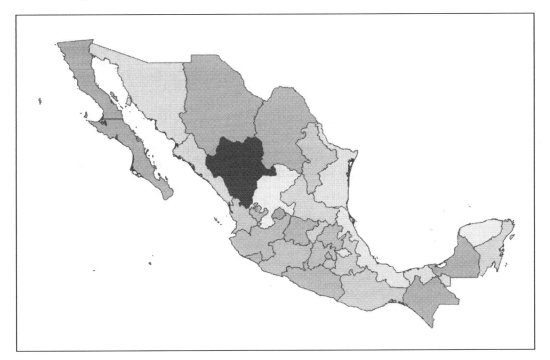

Experiment 4 – using updates and transitions to enhance our visualization

For our next experiment, we will take all of our combined knowledge and add some smooth transitions to the map. Transitions are a fantastic way to add style and smoothness to data changes.

This experiment will, again, require us to start with example-3.html. The complete experiment can be viewed at http://localhost:8080/chapter-4/example-5.html.

If you remember, we leveraged the JavaScript setInterval function to execute updates at a regular timed frequency. We will go back to this method now to assign a random number between 1 and 33 to our existing color function. We will then leverage a D3 method to smoothly transition between the random color changes.

Right below the update section, add the following setInterval block of code:

```
setInterval(function(){
  mexico.transition().duration(500)
      .style('fill', function(d) {
        return color(Math.floor((Math.random() * 32) + 1));
      });
},2000);
```

This method indicates that, for every 2000 milliseconds (2 seconds), the mexico update section should be executed and the color set to a random number between 1 and 32. The new transition and duration methods transition from the previous state to the new state over 500 milliseconds. Open the browser to example-5.html, and you should see the initial color based on the index of the state. After 2 seconds, the colors should smoothly transition to new values.

Experiment 5 – adding points of interest

So far, everything we have done has involved working directly with the geographic data and map. However, there are many cases where you will need to layer additional data on top of the map. We will begin slowly by first adding a few cities of interest to the map of Mexico.

This experiment will, again, require us to start with `example-3.html`. The complete experiment can be viewed at `http://localhost:8080/chapter-4/example-6.html`.

In this experiment, we will add a `text` element to the page to identify the city. To make the text more visually appealing, we will first add some simple styling in the `<style>` section:

```
text{
   font-family: Helvetica;
   font-weight: 300;
   font-size: 12px;
}
```

Next, we need some data that will indicate the city name and the latitude, and longitude coordinates. For the sake of simplicity, we have added a file with a few starter cities. The file called `cities.csv` is in the same directory as the examples:

```
name,lat,lon,
Cancun,21.1606,-86.8475
Mexico City,19.4333,-99.1333
Monterrey,25.6667,-100.3000
Hermosillo,29.0989,-110.9542
```

Now, add a few lines of code to bring in the data and plot the city locations and names on your map. Add the following block of code right below the exit section (if you are starting with `example-2.html`):

```
d3.csv('cities.csv', function(cities) {
   var cityPoints = svg.selectAll('circle').data(cities);
   var cityText = svg.selectAll('text').data(cities);

   cityPoints.enter()
       .append('circle')
       .attr('cx', function(d) {return projection
       ([d.lon, d.lat])[0]})
       .attr('cy', function(d) {return projection
       ([d.lon, d.lat])[1]})
       .attr('r', 4)
```

```
        .attr('fill', 'steelblue');

    cityText.enter()
        .append('text')
        .attr('x', function(d) {return projection
        ([d.lon, d.lat])[0]})
        .attr('y', function(d) {return projection
        ([d.lon, d.lat])[1]})
        .attr('dx', 5)
        .attr('dy', 3)
        .text(function(d) {return d.name});
    });
```

Let's review what we just added.

The `d3.csv` function will make an AJAX call to our data file and automatically format the entire file into an array of JSON objects. Each property of the object will take on the corresponding name of the column in the CSV file. For example, take a look at the following lines of code:

```
[{
  "name": "Cancun",
  "lat":"21.1606",
  "lon":"-86.8475"
}, ...]
```

Next, we will define two variables to hold our "data join" to the circle and text the SVG elements.

Finally, we will execute a typical enter pattern to place the points as circles and the names as text SVG tags on the map. The *x* and *y* coordinates are determined by calling our previous `projection` function with the corresponding latitude and longitude coordinates from the data file.

Note that the `projection` function returns an array of *x* and *y* coordinates (x,y). The *x* coordinate is determined by taking the `0` index of the returned array. The *y* coordinate is determined from the index, `1`. For example, take a look at the following code:

```
.attr('cx', function(d) {return projection([d.lon, d.lat])[0]})
```

Here, `[0]` indicates the *x* coordinate.

Your new map should look like the one shown in the following screenshot:

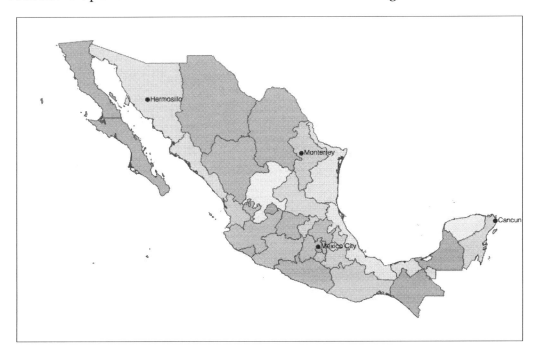

Experiment 6 – adding visualizations as a point of interest

For our final experiment, we will layer visualizations on top of visualizations! Starting from where we left off at `http://localhost:8080/chapter-4/example-6.html`, we will add a fictitious column to the data to indicate a metric of tequila consumption (final version at `http://localhost:8080/chapter-4/example-7.html`):

```
name,lat,lon,tequila
Cancun,21.1606,-86.8475,85,15
Mexico City,19.4333,-99.1333,51,49
Monterrey,25.6667,-100.3000,30,70
Hermosillo,29.0989,-110.9542,20,80
```

With just two more lines of code, we can have the city points portray meaning. In this experiment, we will scale the radius of the city circles in relation to the amount of tequila consumed:

```
var radius = d3.scale.linear().domain([0,100]).range([5,30]);
```

Here, we will introduce a new scale that linearly distributes the input values from 1 to 100 to a radius length between 5 and 30. This means that the minimum radius of a circle will be 5 and the maximum will be 30, preventing the circles from growing too large or too small to be readable:

```
cityPoints.enter()
        .append('circle')
        .attr('cx', function(d) {return projection
        ([d.lon, d.lat])[0];})
        .attr('cy', function(d) {return projection
        ([d.lon, d.lat])[1];})
        .attr('r', 4)
        .attr('fill', 'steelblue');
```

Next, we will change the preceding line of code to call the `radius` function instead of the hard-coded value of 4. The code will now look like this:

```
.attr('r', function(d) {return radius(d.tequila); })
```

After these two small additions, your map should look like the one shown in the following screenshot:

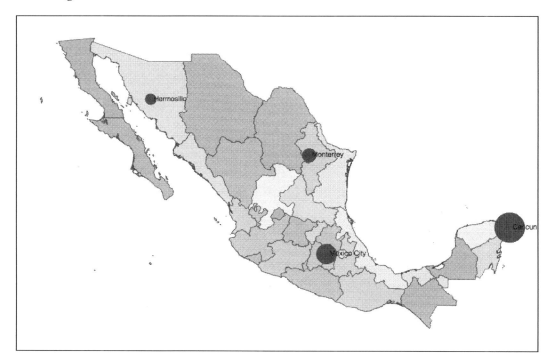

Summary

You learned how to build many different kinds of maps that cover different kinds of needs. Choropleths and data visualizations on maps are some of the most common geographic-based data representations that you will come across. We also added interactivity to our map through basic transitions and events. You will easily realize that, with all the information you've gathered so far, you can independently create engaging map visualizations. You can expand your knowledge by learning advanced interactivity techniques in the next chapter.

Hang on tight!

5

Click-click Boom! Applying Interactivity to Your Map

In the previous chapter, you learned what is needed to build a basic map with D3.js. We also discussed the concepts of enter, update, and exit and how they apply to maps. You should also understand how D3 mix-and-matches HTML with data. However, let's say you want to take it a step further and include more interaction on your map. We covered just the tip of the iceberg with click events in the previous chapter. Now, it's time to dig deeper.

In this chapter, we will expand our knowledge of events and event types. We will progress experiment by experiment, building on what we've learned. The following topics are covered in this chapter:

- Events and how they occur
- Experiment 1 – hover events and tooltips
- Experiment 2 – tooltips with visualizations
- Experiment 3 – panning and zooming
- Experiment 4 – orthographic projections
- Experiment 5 – rotating orthographic projections
- Experiment 6 – dragging orthographic projections

Events and how they occur

Taken directly from the w3 specifications:

> *"The Event interface is used to provide contextual information about an event to the handler processing the event. An object that implements the Event interface is generally passed as the first parameter to an event handler. More specific context information is passed to event handlers by deriving additional interfaces from Event which contain information directly relating to the type of event they accompany. These derived interfaces are also implemented by the object passed to the event listener."*

In other words, an event is an action that takes place in your browser by user input. If your user clicks, touches, drags, and rotates, an event will fire. If you have event listeners registered to those particular events, the listeners will catch the event and determine the event type. The listeners will also expose properties associated with the event. For example, if we want to add an event listener in plain JavaScript, we would add the following lines of code:

```
<body>
  <button id="btn">Click me</button>

  <script>
    varbtn = document.getElementById('btn');
    btn.addEventListener('click', function() {
      console.log('Hello world'); }, false );
  </script>
</body>
```

Note that you first need to have the button in the DOM in order to get its ID. Once you have it, you can simply add an event listener to listen on the element's click event. The event listener will catch the click event every time it fires and log `Hello world` into the console.

Up until jQuery, events were very tricky, and different browsers had different ways of catching these events. However, thankfully, this is all in the past. Now, we live in a world where modern browsers are more consistent with event handling.

In the world of D3, you won't have to worry about this. Generating events, catching them, and reacting to them is baked into the library and works across all browsers. A good example of this is the hover event.

Experiment 1 – hover events

Building on our previous example, we can easily swap our `click` method into a `hover` method. Instead of having `var click`, we will now have `var hover` with the corresponding function. Feel free to open `example-1.html` of the `chapter-5` code base to go over the complete example (`http://localhost:8080/chapter-5/example-1.html`). Let's review the changes necessary to change our click event to a hover event. In this particular case, we will need a little more CSS and HTML. In our `<style>` tag, add the following lines:

```
#tooltip{
position: absolute;
z-index: 2;
background: rgba(0,153,76,0.8);
width:130px;
height:20px;
color:white;
font-size: 14px;
padding:5px;
top:-150px;
left:-150px;
font-family: "HelveticaNeue-Light", "Helvetica Neue Light",
"Helvetica Neue", Helvetica, Arial, "Lucida Grande", sans-serif;
}
```

This style is for a basic tooltip. It is positioned "absolutely" so that it can take whatever *x* and *y* coordinates we give it (left and top). It also has some filler styles for the fonts and colors. The tooltip is styled to the element in the DOM that has the ID of `#tooltip`:

```
<div id="tooltip"></div>
```

Next, we want to add the logic to handle a hover event when it is fired:

```
var hover = function(d) {
  var div = document.getElementById('tooltip');
  div.style.left = event.pageX +'px';
  div.style.top = event.pageY + 'px';
  div.innerHTML = d.properties.NAME_1;
};
```

This function, aside from logging the event, will find the DOM element with an ID of `tooltip` and position it to the *x* and *y* coordinates of the event. These coordinates are part of the properties of the event and are named `pageX` and `pageY`, respectively. Next, we will insert text with the state name (`d.properties.NAME_1`) into the tooltip:

```
//Enter
mexico.enter()
   .append('path')
   .attr('d', path)
   .on("mouseover", hover);
```

Finally, we will change our binding from a click to a mouseover event in the on section of the code. We will also change the event handler to the `hover` function we created earlier.

Once the changes have been saved and viewed, you should experience basic tooltips on your map:

Experiment 2 – tooltips with visualizations

In this next experiment, we will enhance our tooltips with additional visualizations. In a similar fashion, we will outline the additional code to provide this functionality (http://localhost:8080/chapter-5/example-2.html).

To our CSS, we will need to add the following lines of code:

```
#tooltip svg{
border-top:0;
margin-left:-5px;
margin-top:7px;
}
```

This will style our SVG container (inside our tooltip DOM element) to align it with the label of the state.

Next, we'll include two new scripts to create visualizations:

```
<script src="base.js"></script>
<script src="sparkline.js"></script>
```

The preceding JavaScript files contain the D3 code that creates a line chart visualization. The chart itself contains and leverages the *reusable chart pattern* described by Mike Bostock at http://bost.ocks.org/mike/chart/. Feel free to examine the code; it is a very simple visualization that follows the enter, update, and exit pattern. We will explore this chart further in *Chapter 7, Testing*:

```
var db = d3.map();
var sparkline = d3.charts.sparkline().height(50).width(138);
```

We will now declare two new variables. The db variable will hold a hashmap to quickly lookup values by geoID. The sparkline variable is the function that will draw our simple line chart:

```
var setDb = function(data) {
  data.forEach(function(d) {
    db.set(d.geoID, [
        {"x": 1, "y": +d.q1},
        {"x": 2, "y": +d.q2},
        {"x": 3, "y": +d.q3},
        {"x": 4, "y": +d.q4}
    ]);
  });
};
```

This function parses data and formats it into a structure that the sparkline function can use to create the line chart:

```
var geoID = function(d) {
  return "c" + d.properties.ID_1;
};
```

We will bring back our geoID function from *Chapter 4, Creating a Map,* in order to quickly create unique IDs for each state:

```
var hover = function(d) {
  var div = document.getElementById('tooltip');
  div.style.left = event.pageX +'px';
  div.style.top = event.pageY + 'px';
  div.innerHTML = d.properties.NAME_1;

  var id = geoID(d);
  d3.select("#tooltip").datum(db.get(id)).call(sparkline.draw);
};
```

For our hover event handler, we need to add two new lines. First, we will declare an ID variable that holds the unique geoID for the state we are hovering over. Then, we will call our sparkline function to draw a line chart in the tooltip selection. The data is retrieved from the preceding db variable. For more information on how the call works, refer to https://developer.mozilla.org/en-US/docs/Web/JavaScript/Reference/Global_Objects/Function/call:

```
d3.csv('states-data.csv', function(data) {
  setDb(data);
});
```

We load our CSV file via AJAX and invoke the setDb function (described earlier).

You should now see a map that displays a tooltip with a line chart for every state in Mexico. In summary:

1. The map is drawn as usual.
2. We will create a small lookup db that contains additional data about each state.
3. Then, we will register a hover event that fires whenever the user's mouse passes over a state.
4. The hover event fires and retrieves data about the state.

5. The hover event also places the name of the state in the DOM and calls a function that creates a line chart with the retrieved data.

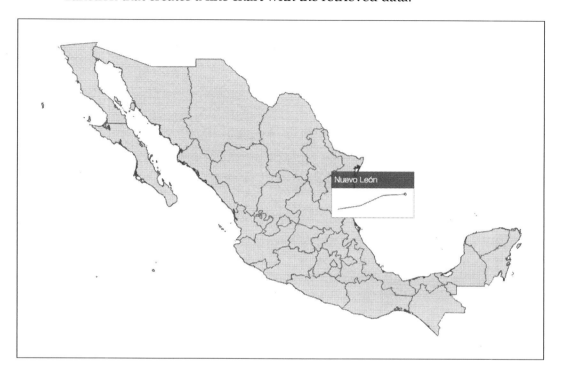

Experiment 3 – panning and zooming

A very common request when working with maps is to provide the ability to pan and zoom around the visualization. This is especially useful when a large map contains abundant detail. Luckily, D3 provides an event listener to help with this feature. In this experiment, we will outline the principles to provide basic panning and zooming for your map. This experiment requires us to start with `example-1. html`; however, feel free to look at `http://localhost:8080/chapter-5/ example-3.html` for reference.

First, we will add a simple CSS class in our `<style>` section; this class will act as a rectangle over the entire map. This will be our zoomable area:

```
.overlay {
fill: none;
pointer-events: all;
}
```

Next, we need to define a function to handle the event when the zoom listener is fired. The following function can be placed right below the map declaration:

```
var zoomed = function () {
  map.attr("transform", "translate("+ d3.event.translate + ")
  scale(" + d3.event.scale + ")");
};
```

This function takes advantage of two variables exposed while panning and zooming: `d3.event.scale` and `d3.event.translate`. The variables are defined as follows:

- `d3.event.scale`: This defines how much the user has zoomed in terms of an SVG scale

- `d3.event.translate`: This defines the position of the map in relation to the mouse in terms of an SVG translate

With this information available, we can set the SVG attributes (scale and translate) of the map container to the event variables:

```
var zoom = d3.behavior.zoom()
    .scaleExtent([1, 8])
    .on("zoom", zoomed);
    .size([width, height]);
```

Similar to the hover event listener, we need to create a new zoom event listener. Create the preceding function after the `zoom` function. Note that there is one additional setting to understand, `scaleExtent`.

The `scaleExtent` setting provides a scale range of the zooming amount. The first element in the array is the maximum that the map can zoom out. The second element in the array is the maximum that the map can zoom in. Remember that 1 is the original size of our map based on our bounding-box formula from *Chapter 4, Creating a Map*. The minimum value that `scaleExtent` can be set to is 0 to zoom out. In `example-3. html`, alter these numbers to get a feel of how they work. For example, if you change 1 to 5, you will see that the map can zoom out to half its original size.

There are additional settings to this event listener that can be reviewed at `https://github.com/mbostock/d3/wiki/Zoom-Behavior`:

```
svg.append("rect")
      .attr("class", "overlay")
      .attr("width", width)
      .attr("height", height)
      .call(zoom);
```

Finally, right after the `mexico.exit` section, we will add a transparent rectangle to the entire visualization and bind the new listener. Remember that the rectangle is using the CSS class we defined at the beginning of the experiment.

Now, you should have full zoomming and panning capabilities on the Mexican map. You can either double-click to zoom in or use your scroll wheel. The interactions should also work across swipe and pinch gestures on a tablet.

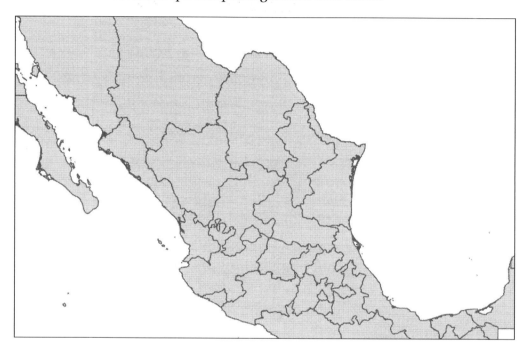

Experiment 4 – orthographic projections

For the next set of experiments in this chapter, we will switch gears and look at interactivity with orthographic projections (representing a three-dimensional map on a two-dimensional screen). A better visualization to illustrate these concepts is the entire globe instead of a single country. This experiment will start with `http://localhost:8080/chapter-5/example-4.html` and require a new datafile, which is provided for you. You will notice that the code base is almost identical, with the exception of three changes that we will outline here:

```
var height = 600;
var width = 900;
var projection = d3.geo.orthographic().clipAngle(90);
var path = d3.geo.path().projection(projection);
```

First, we will change our d3.geo projection from d3.geo.mercator to d3.geo. orthographic. We also have an additional setting to configure: the clipAngle at 90 degrees. This places an imaginary plane through the globe and clips the back of the projection:

```
d3.json('world.json', function(data) {
var countries = topojson.feature(data, data.objects.countries);
var map = svg.append('g').attr('class', 'boundary');
var world = map.selectAll('path').data(countries.features);
```

Next, we will substitute the old geo-data.json file for the new datafile, world. json. We will also set up new variables for our data joining in order to provide better readability in the code:

```
world.enter()
      .append('path')
      .attr('d', path);
```

As we have seen many times now, we will apply the standard enter pattern. You should now have a static map of the globe, as seen in the following screenshot. You can also work directly with example-4.html.

In the last two sections, we will bring the globe to life!

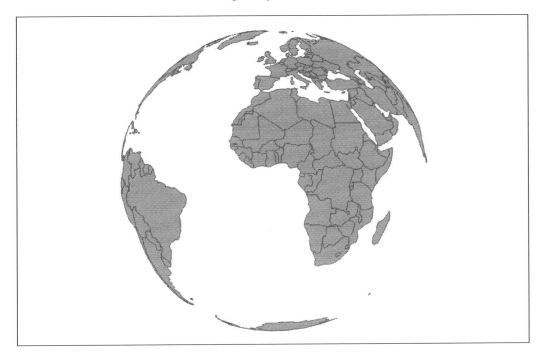

Experiment 5 – rotating orthographic projections

Our previous example was very fascinating. We went from visualizing a map in two dimensions to three dimensions in just a few lines. The next step is to animate it. For this experiment, open `http://localhost:8080/chapter-5/example-5.html` in the code samples. Let's now piece it together:

```
var i = 0;
```

We added an index variable that will hold the rotation rate. Don't worry; we'll explain how this is used here:

```
d3.json('world.json', function(data) {
var countries = topojson.feature(data, data.objects.countries);
var mexico = countries.features[102];
```

As Mexico is the center of the universe and requires special attention, we isolated it into its own variable by taking the corresponding feature from the countries feature array. This will allow us to manipulate it separately from the rest of the globe:

```
var map = svg.append('g').attr('class', 'boundary');
var world = map.selectAll('path').data(countries.features);
var mexico = map.selectAll('.mexico').data([mexico]);
```

Next, we will *data join* the information we isolated earlier into its own variable. This way, we will have one map that represents the entire world and another one that represents just Mexico:

```
mexico.enter()
  .append('path')
  .attr('class', 'mexico')
  .attr('d', path)
  .style('fill', 'lightyellow').style('stroke', 'orange');
```

We will inject the map of Mexico and apply the identical `geo.path` that contains the same projection as the one used for the world map. We will also add a light yellow background to Mexico using the `fill` CSS style and an orange border using the stroke:

```
setInterval(function() {
i = i+0.2;
    // move i around in the array to get a feel for yaw, pitch
    // and roll
    // see diagram
projection.rotate([i,0,0])
```

```
world.attr('d', path);
mexico.attr('d', path)
   .style('fill', 'lightyellow').style('stroke', 'orange');
      }, 20);
```

This is where the action gets moving, literally. We created an interval that executes every 20 milliseconds. This interval contains a function that utilizes our index variable and increments the value by 0.2. This value is then applied to the `rotate` function of our projection. Specifically, we will adjust the rotation every 20 ms on this line of code:

```
projection.rotate([i,0,0])
```

Yaw is represented by the first value of the array (in this case, `i`), pitch by the second value, and roll by the third value. Yaw, pitch, and roll are rotation angles and are applied in their respective vectors. The following image provides an illustration of how the angles rotate:

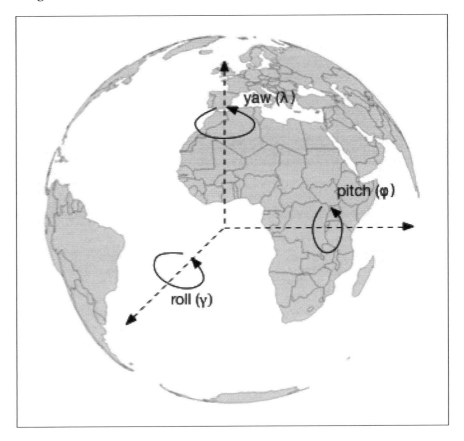

Here, we see that the yaw vector points in the z direction and is around the center axis. The pitch goes along our x axis, and the yaw goes around our y axis. The Greek characters, in parenthesis in the preceding image, are often used to depict yaw, pitch, and roll.

In our case, the index variable i is increasing and is allocated to the yaw rotation. This means that our globe will spin from left to right around the center axis. If we were to swap the position of our index so it is in the pitch location (the second array element), our globe would spin vertically:

```
project.rotate([0,i,0]);
```

Finally, we will use the same D3 update pattern and update all the paths with the new projection. Give it a shot, play around with the example, and see how the globe spins in different directions. When complete, you will see the globe rotating globe in your browser, as in the following screenshot:

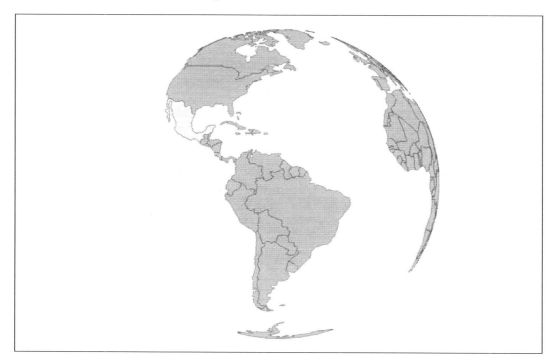

Experiment 6 – dragging orthographic projections

For our last example, we will add the ability to drag our globe so that the user can spin it to the left or right. Open `http://localhost:8080/chapter-5/example-6.html` from the code samples and let's get started:

```
var dragging = function(d) {
var c = projection.rotate();
projection.rotate([c[0] + d3.event.dx/2, c[1], c[2]])

world.attr('d', path);
mexico.attr('d', path)
        .style('fill', 'lightyellow').style('stroke', 'orange');
};
```

Our first piece of new code is our dragging event handler. This function will be executed every time the user drags the mouse on the screen. The algorithm executes the following steps:

1. Store the current rotation value.
2. Update the projection's rotation based on the amount `dragged`.
3. Update all the paths in the world map.
4. Update all the paths in the map of Mexico.

The second step deserves a little more explanation. Just like the `d3.behavior.zoom` event handler, `d3.behavior.drag` exposes information about the performed action. In this case, `d3.event.dx` and `d3.event.dy` indicate the distance dragged from the previous location. The `c[0] + d3.event.dx/2` code tells us that we need to take the previous yaw value and add the amount of drag the user is performing. We will divide the drag amount by 2 to slow down the rotation by half; otherwise, every pixel the user drags will correlate to 1 degree of rotation:

```
var drag = d3.behavior.drag()
    .on("drag", dragging);
```

Next, we will bind our `dragging` method to our drag event, as we saw earlier, with click, hover, and zoom:

```
svg.append("rect")
        .attr("class", "overlay")
        .attr("width", width)
        .attr("height", height)
        .call(drag);
```

Finally, we need an area to bind our drag event. Using our previous technique, we will add a transparent rectangle on top of the visualization. This will allow us to very clearly detect the *x* and *y* positions on our SVG element.

Give it a spin! You'll notice that if you click-and-drag the world, it will spin in the corresponding yaw direction.

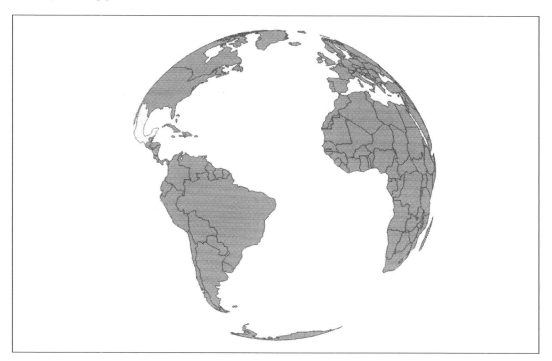

Summary

We covered many examples to get you started with interactivity in your D3 map visualizations. We went over the basics of event handling, explored various methods to bind events to the map, outlined the two `d3.behavior` APIs, and even dipped our toes into orthographic projections. If you wish to dig deeper into world rotations, and the math involved, check out the Jason Davies article at `http://www.jasondavies.com/maps/rotate/`.

After two chapters of drawing and interacting with maps, the next chapter will explain how to obtain geo data in order to create any map you want. We'll also include some techniques to optimize the datafiles for viewing the Web.

6
Finding and Working with Geographic Data

We have spent significant time creating and interacting with maps in our previous chapters. In all our examples, the geographic data was included. In this chapter, we will explain how to find geographic data about any country in the world.

There are typically two sets of data that we will need to create a map in D3:

- A dataset that represents the geographic shape of our map (geo data)
- Some meaningful data that we want to visualize on the map (for example, population density by US counties or unemployment rate by countries in the world)

This chapter is focused on understanding, manipulating, and optimizing geo data for map visualizations. We will accomplish these goals by:

- Explaining three important formats that contain geospatial vector data
- Finding, downloading, and working with large amounts of map data
- Using techniques to build the right geo data file for your map

GeoData file types

There are dozens of file formats that represent geographic information. In this section, we will focus on three file types: shapefiles, GeoJSON, and TopoJSON.

What are shapefiles and how do I get them?

Shapefiles are the most popular vector-based file format. They contain polygons and lines that represent geographic boundaries. The shapefile format was developed by the company Esri as an open standard to work with **Geographic Information Systems (GIS)**. This vector information can also describe other geographic entities (rivers, lakes, and railroads). In addition, the file format has the ability to store data attributes that are useful when working with visualizations (for example, the name of the geographic object, the type, and some relationships). Most importantly for us, there is a large repository of free shapefiles located at `http://diva-gis.org`. This repository contains a tremendous wealth of data at different levels of specificity and granularity.

Unfortunately for us, shapefiles are in binary format and can be very large. This makes them very difficult, if not impossible, to use in standard web development. Thankfully, there are some tools to help us leverage the large repository of shapefiles and convert them to GeoJSON and TopoJSON. GeoJSON and TopoJSON are JavaScript-friendly, much smaller, and easier to use in our web development context. In the previous chapters, all of the geographic data was provided in TopoJSON.

Acquiring shapefiles for a specific country

Let's start with a map of Spain and go through the process of getting our first shapefile:

1. Go to `http://www.diva-gis.org/gdata` and select **Spain** from the drop-down list as shown in the following screenshot:

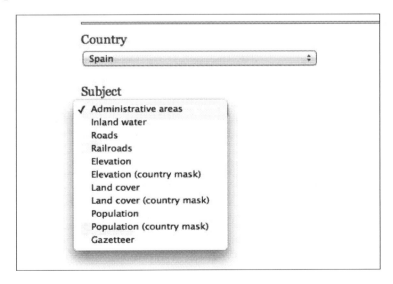

2. Once **Spain** is selected, you will see a large selection of geographic data to choose from (**Roads, Railroads**, and so on). Select the **Administrative areas** option to draw the primary boundaries of the country and regions. Click on **OK**; it will take you to the download page.

3. Once it's downloaded, you will have an `ESP_adm.zip` file containing the shapefile data for the administrative areas of Spain.

4. After unzipping the file, you will see that the files are organized into progressively increasing numbers—`ESP_adm0` to `ESP_adm4`. ESP represents the abbreviation of the country and each number represents the increasing amount of detail found in each data file.

   For example, `ESP_adm0` will draw just the outline of Spain, while `ESP_adm3` will include the provinces of the country.

GeoJSON

GeoJSON is a specific JSON format for describing geographic data structures. It is important to know that GeoJSON:

- Contains all the information required to draw geographic data.

- Is a standard JSON format and can be used instantly in JavaScript when building for the Web.

- Is required by D3 when defining our `d3.geo.path` function, as seen in the previous chapters.

- Discretely defines each geographic shape. For example, if two countries share a border, the GeoJSON file will completely define both countries, therefore defining the border twice. It does not provide any mechanisms to optimize the datafile.

Because D3 relies on GeoJSON, we will explain some of the highlights of the specification. For a complete explanation please see `http://geojson.org`.

Typically, you will not incorporate the GeoJSON file directly in your D3 work. TopoJSON, explained in the next section, offers a more compact solution. However, it is still important to understand the specification so let's walk through the GeoJSON of Spain:

```
{
    "type": "FeatureCollection",
    "features": [
        {
            "type": "Feature",
            "properties": {
```

```
        "GADMID": 70,
        "ISO": "ESP",
        "NAME_ENGLI": "Spain",
        "NAME_ISO": "SPAIN",
        "NAME_FAO": "Spain",
        "NAME_LOCAL": "España",
        ...
    },
    "geometry": {
        "type": "MultiPolygon",
        "coordinates": [
            [
                [
                    [
                        0.518472,
                        40.53236
                    ],
                    [
                        0.518194,
                        40.53236
                    ],
                    ...
                ]
            ]
        ]
    }
]
}
```

The first property of the JSON object identifies the GeoJSON file as a collection of features (`FeatureCollection`). Each member of the collection (the array in the preceding `features` property) holds a specially formatted JSON object called a feature. The `d3.geo.path` function that we used in the previous chapters knows how to convert the `feature` object into a polygon using an SVG path. By iterating over an array of these features and drawing each polygon one by one, we create a D3 map.

The `feature` object must adhere to the following properties in order for D3 to convert the object into a polygon:

- `geometry`: This is another GeoJSON specification that contains types and coordinates that indicate exactly how to draw the shape. We will not spend a lot of time explaining exactly how the specification draws the object. D3 will do all the hard work for us. Leveraging the enter/update/exit pattern, we pass a special `d3.geo.path` function to each feature. This function will take the geometry information about the feature and create the shape for us automatically.

- `properties`: This is any additional data to be attached to the feature. This is a typical name/value pair JSON object. In the preceding example, the `properties` attribute is leveraged to store the name of the country. This is very helpful when we need to find the country later to bind additional data to the visualization. See the following screenshot for examples of properties that can be bound to a feature object:

```
▼ 1: Object
  ▶ geometry: Object
  ▼ properties: Object
      CC_1: "02"
      ENGTYPE_1: "Autonomous Community"
      HASC_1: "ES.AR"
      ID_0: 70
      ID_1: 936
      ISO: "ESP"
      NAME_0: "Spain"
      NAME_1: "Aragón"
      NL_NAME_1: null
      REMARKS_1: null
      Shape_Area: 5.15083538648
      Shape_Leng: 15.0953070773
      TYPE_1: "Comunidad Autónoma"
      VALIDFR_1: "1982"
      VALIDTO_1: "Present"
      VARNAME_1: "Aragão|Aragó|Aragón|Aragona|Aragonien"
    ▶ __proto__: Object
    type: "Feature"
  ▶ __proto__: Object
```

- `id`: This is a place holder that can be leveraged to store a unique identifier to the particular feature in the collection.

A quick map in D3 with only GeoJSON

For a moment, let's pretend that TopoJSON does not exist and illustrate how only GeoJSON can be used to create a map. This will help illustrate the need for TopoJSON in the next section. The following code snippet is a quick example to tie everything together; you can also open `example-1.html` from the `chapter-6` folder (`http://localhost:8080/chapter-6/example-1.html`) to see the map in your browser:

```
d3.json('geojson/spain-geo.json', function(data) {
  var b, s, t;
  projection.scale(1).translate([0, 0]);
  var b = path.bounds(data);
  var s = .9 / Math.max((b[1][0] - b[0][0]) / width,
  (b[1][1] - b[0][1]) / height);
  var t = [(width - s * (b[1][0] + b[0][0])) / 2,
  (height - s * (b[1][1] + b[0][1])) / 2];
  projection.scale(s).translate(t);

  map = svg.append('g').attr('class', 'boundary');
  spain = map.selectAll('path').data(data.features);
```

Notice that the code is almost identical to the examples in the previous chapters. The only exception is that we are not calling the `topojson` function (we will cover why `topojson` is important next). Instead, we are passing the data from the AJAX call directly into the *data join* for the following `enter` call:

```
spain.enter()
    .append('path')
    .attr('d', path);

});
```

As predicted, we have our map of Spain:

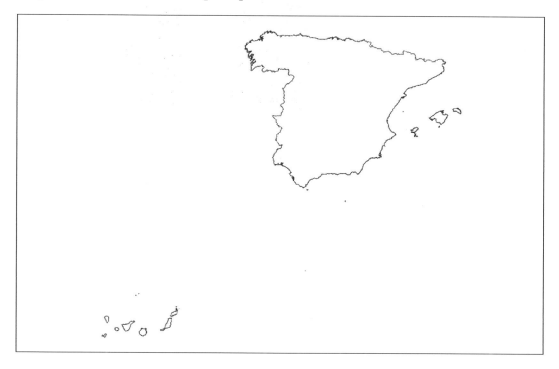

While using GeoJSON directly may seem like the best approach, there are some problems. Primarily, a one-to-one conversion of an ESRI shapefile to the GeoJSON format contains a lot of detail that is probably unnecessary and will create a huge GeoJSON file. The larger the file, the more time it will take to download. For example, `spain-geo.json` produced an almost 7 MB GeoJSON file.

Next, we will explore how TopoJSON can help by modifying several optimization levers while still maintaining significant details.

TopoJSON basics

TopoJSON is another JSON-based format that encodes geographic data. If you remember, GeoJSON describes geographic data discretely. This means GeoJSON borders can be described twice. The TopoJSON format removes this duplicate behavior, often creating files that are 80 percent smaller. This format is extremely helpful when building for the Web, where data transfer size plays an important role.

The term TopoJSON can be confusing. Let's break it down into its three dimensions:

- **TopoJSON, the serialized format**: The actual serialized-JSON format that describes how to draw geographic shapes.

- **topojson, the command line utility**: This is a program that a user can run to create TopoJSON files from shapefiles. The utility contains many levers to further reduce the size of the file.

- **topojson.js, the JavaScript library**: The library used in your D3 map to convert the TopoJSON-serialized format back to GeoJSON so that the `d3.geo.path` functions work correctly.

To illustrate to what extent TopoJSON can reduce the file size, let's execute the command-line utility against the shapefiles we downloaded earlier. Open the command line and execute the following in the same directory where you downloaded and unzipped the `ESP_adm.zip` file:

```
topojson -o spain-topo.json -p -- ESP_adm0.shp
```

This command creates a new topojson-formatted file named `spain-topo.json` and preserves all the data properties (the `-p` flag) from the `ESP_adm0` shapefile (note that the shapefile needs to come after the `--` in the command-line syntax). The `-o` parameter defines the name of the resulting topojson file.

First, let's compare file sizes with GeoJSON versus TopoJSON for the exact same geographic region:

- GeoJSON: 6.4 MB
- TopoJSON: 379 KB

This is an incredible compression rate, and we just used the defaults!

In order to incorporate TopoJSON into our map, we need to use the `topojson.js` JavaScript library and alter a few lines of code. We will start with `example-1.html`. The final version can be viewed in `example-2.html` (`http://localhost:8080/chapter-6/example-2.html`).

```
<script src="http://d3js.org/topojson.v1.min.js"></script>
```

First, we add the JavaScript library as a `<script>` tag to our file. Now you know why we have been using this library all along.

```
d3.json('topojson/spain-topo.json', function(data) {
```

Next, we inject our topojson file that we just created via AJAX.

```
var country = topojson.feature(data, data.objects.ESP_adm0);
```

We add an additional line of code to convert the TopoJSON format to the GeoJSON feature format.

```
var b = path.bounds(country);
```

We need to remember to create our bounding box using the interpolated features.

```
spain = map.selectAll('path').data(country.features);
```

Now, we use the *data join* on our new data. As expected, we will see our map of Spain. Let's show them side-by-side in the following screenshot to compare GeoJSON and TopoJSON (GeoJSON on the left and TopoJSON on the right):

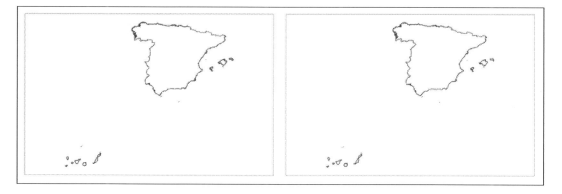

TopoJSON command-line tips

The topojson command-line documentation is very complete (`https://github.com/mbostock/topojson/wiki/Command-Line-Reference`). However, here are a couple of quick and easy tips to get you started.

Preserving specific attributes

In the *GeoJSON* section, we illustrated that data properties are often part of the geographic data. The `topojson` command gives you the ability to filter out the ones you are not interested in, as well as provide a better naming convention to the ones you do want to keep. These capabilities are in the `-p` flag and passed to the command. For example:

```
topojson -o spain-topo.json -p name=ISO -- ESP_adm0.shp
```

We will create the topojson file, remove all properties except ISO, and rename the ISO property to something easy to recognize—name. You can address multiple properties by commas separating the list:

```
-p target=source,target=source,target=source
```

Simplification

Mike Bostock provides an excellent tutorial on simplification and how it works at `http://bost.ocks.org/mike/simplify/`.

Basically, it is a way to reduce geometric complexity through line simplification algorithms. For example, if you do not need much detail in a very jagged coast of a country, you can apply line simplification algorithms to smooth out the jaggedness and significantly reduce the size of the TopoJSON file. The command-line parameter you use is `-s` to adjust the simplification in the TopoJSON conversion.

```
-p  name=ISO -s 7e-7 -- ESP_adm0.shp
```

We typically realize that when dealing with shapefiles from DIVA-GIS, the best range is around 7e-7 to keep within the per-pixel threshold, which is less than the area of the map. At this range, the size compression is very significant and the map quality is still very acceptable for web development. Consider the following:

- **Original**: 378 KB, great detail and quality:

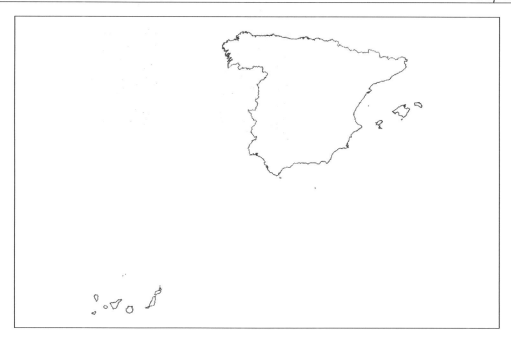

- **Simplified at -s 7e-7**: 3.6 KB and acceptable quality:

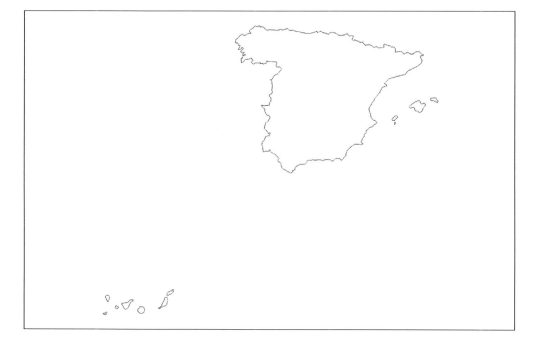

- **Very Simple at –s 7e-5**: 568 bytes but the map is unrecognizable:

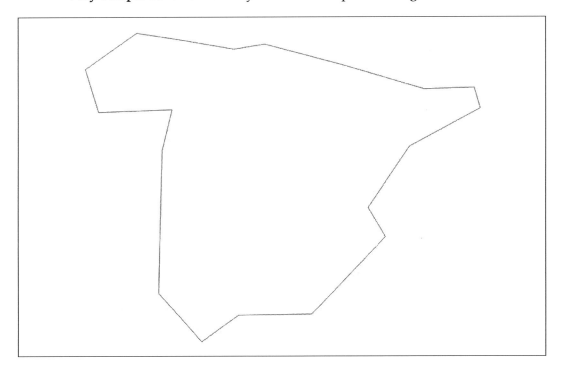

Merging files

The final tip involves merging multiple shapefiles into a single TopoJSON file. This is extremely useful if you need separate geographic information but want to fetch it in a single AJAX request. To append additional files, you add them after the – in the command line.

Consider this command:

```
topojson -o ../topojson/spain-topo-simple.json -p  name=ISO -s 7e-7 -
- ESP_adm0.shp ESP_adm1.shp
```

It will produce the following object structure, where the data for `ESP_adm0` is the data for the country and `ESP_adm1` is the data for the regions:

```
data ▼ Object {type: "Topology", objects: Objec
        ▶ arcs: Array[285]
        ▼ objects: Object
          ▶ ESP_adm0: Object
          ▶ ESP_adm1: Object
          ▶ __proto__: Object
        ▶ transform: Object
          type: "Topology"
        ▶ __proto__: Object
```

There is also the opportunity to rename the object they will map to in the resulting TopoJSON file. Again, this can help create readable code. The renaming follows the same convention as renaming specific properties. For example, type in this command:

```
topojson -o ../topojson/spain-topo-simple.json -p  name=ISO -s 7e-7 -
- country=ESP_adm0.shp regions=ESP_adm1.shp
```

The preceding command will create the following:

```
▼ Object {type: "Topology", objec
    ▶ arcs: Array[285]
    ▼ objects: Object
      ▶ country: Object
      ▶ regions: Object
      ▶ __proto__: Object
    ▶ transform: Object
      type: "Topology"
    ▶ __proto__: Object
```

In this case, you would change your original code, which is as follows:

```
var country = topojson.feature(data, data.objects.ESP_adm0);
```

You have to change it to the following code:

```
var country = topojson.feature(data, data.objects.country);
```

This is much nicer to look at! Please look at example-3.html (http://localhost:8080/chapter-6/example-3.html) to see how all of this information can be tied together.

Summary

At this point, you should feel confident that you can find and modify datasets to your needs. We've covered common locations from where you can acquire data and we've touched on the different types of flags topojson offers. With these skills, it is up to you to make sure your data is trimmed and is acquired to your visualization needs. This closes the circle of developing maps with D3. In the next chapter, we will refine your craft by focusing on testing your visualizations.

7
Testing

In this chapter, we will cover several topics that will assist you in the long-term maintenance of your D3 code base. The goal is to create a foundation to build reusable assets that can be easily unit tested while leveraging popular tools and techniques already established in the JavaScript community.

Unit testing is important in any software development project, especially in a D3 code base. Typically, these projects involve a lot of code that applies analytics or manipulates data structures. For these types of problems, unit testing can help in the following ways:

- **Reduce bugs**: An automated test suite will allow the developer to break down and test individual components. These tests will be run constantly throughout the development cycle, validating that future features do not break older working code.

- **Document accurately**: Often, tests are written in a human-readable way; this precisely describes the problem they are testing against. An example of the code provides much better documentation than a long paragraph.

- **Allow refactoring**: The developer can change code semantics and design with confidence, knowing that the inputs and outputs are still tracked and validated.

- **Make development faster**: Most developers spend time validating their work as they write. We've seen developers tirelessly refresh browsers, check console logs, and inspect DOM elements as they go. Instead of performing these manual actions over and over again, simply wrap them up in a framework that does the work for you.

This chapter will explore a project bootstrap that we like to use when starting a new visualization development. The concepts covered in the start project include:

- Project structure
- Code organization and reusable assets
- Unit testing
- A resilient code base

Code organization and reusable assets

The foundation of our way of writing reusable and testable D3 code is from Mike Bostock's blog article, *Towards Reusable Charts*, at http://bost.ocks.org/mike/chart/. It is actually a great idea to read this article before continuing, as we can take some of our career experiences and extend these concepts a little further. The project structure is organized to achieve several goals.

Project structure

The bootstrap project contains the following files and directories:

The project works out-of-the-box with example code already in place. To see this in action, we will launch the example. From the example bootstrap code provided, first, install all the dependencies (note that you only have to execute this command once):

```
npm install
```

Then, to see the visualization, execute this:

```
node node_modules/http-server/bin/http-server
```

Next, open the browser to `http://localhost:8080`. You should see three bars changing based on random data in a series of tests. Note that if you have the previous examples already open, you will have to kill that process in order to run this one, as both of them use the same port.

To see the unit tests working, just execute this:

node_modules/karma/bin/karma start

You should see a summary of five unit tests running in the terminal and a continuing running process monitoring your project:

```
INFO [karma]: Karma v0.12.21 server started at
http://localhost:9876/
INFO [launcher]: Starting browser Chrome
INFO [Chrome 37.0.2062 (Mac OS X 10.9.5)]: Connected on socket
goMqmrnZkxyz9nlpQHem with id 16699326
Chrome 37.0.2062 (Mac OS X 10.9.5): Executed 5 of 5 SUCCESS
(0.018 secs / 0.013 secs)
```

We will explain how to write unit tests for the project later in this chapter. For a quick peek at what tests are running, look at `spec/viz_spec.js`.

If you change any of the methods in this file, you will notice that the test runner will detect that a change has been made in the code and re-execute the tests! This provides a fantastic feedback loop to the developer as you continue to enhance your work.

Exploring the code directory

In this section, we will cover each file in detail and explain its importance in the overall package:

- `index.html`: This file is the starting point of the visualization and will launch automatically when you point your browser to `http://localhost:8080`. You will notice that the file contains many of the points already covered in the book in terms of loading up the proper assets. As we walk through `index.html`, we will identify the other directories and files used in the project.

- `main.css`: The `main.css` file is used to apply specific CSS styling to your visualization:

```
<link rel="stylesheet" type="text/css" href="main.css">
```

- `vendor`: This directory contains all the external libraries that we need to use in the visualization and is loaded at the bottom of the `index.html` file:

```
<script src="vendor/d3.min.js"></script>
<script src="vendor/topojson.v1.min.js"></script>
```

  We like to keep these to a minimum so that we have as few dependencies to the outside world as possible. In this case, we are only using the core D3 library and topojson to help us with the GeoJSON encoding.

- `scripts`: This is another directory; there are some new additions to the files we are loading in order to create the visualization.:

```
<!-- A base function for setting up the SVG and container -->
<script src="scripts/base.js"></script>


<!-- The main visualization code -->
<script src="scripts/viz.js"></script>
```

  The `base.js` script contains some common D3 patterns that are reused in many examples (such as containing the visualization in a chart area `<g>` with a predefined margin object, common methods to calculate height and width based on this margin object, and a handy utility to find the existing container and binding data). The `base.js` script is also an excellent location to keep reusable code.

  The `viz.js` script is an example that leverages many of the concepts in Towards Reusable Charts with some inheritance gained from `base.js`. The `viz.js` script is the workhorse of the project and where most of the visualization code will reside.

- `factories`: This too is the directory. In order to show our work in the browser, we need a script to generate some data, select the element in the DOM, and initiate the visualization call. These scripts are organized in the `factories` directory. An example of this can be viewed in the `viz_factory.js` file:

```
<!-- The script acts as a proxy to call the visualization
and draw it with sample data -->
<script src="factories/viz_factory.js"></script>
```

- `spec`: The tests you write to validate the methods in the visualization code go here. A detailed example will be provided later in this chapter.

Other administrative files

Two additional files that assist with the operation of the bootstrap project are as follows; these files rarely require any modification:

- `karma.conf.js`: This is used to set up the unit test runs
- `package.json`: This describes which npm packages to install

Writing testable code

There are dozens of factors to consider when creating visualizations. Every design will have its own set of unique requirements and configuration capabilities to consider. If you build on the reusable pattern outlined by Mike Bostock, you will have a great framework to start with.

When working with data visualizations, we will have some form of data manipulation or logic that must be applied to incoming data. There are two notable best practices we can leverage to test and validate these operations. They are explained in the following sections.

Keeping methods/functions small

Small functions mean low cyclomatic complexity. This means there are fewer logic branches in each function and, therefore, fewer things to test. If we test each simple function thoroughly and independently, then there will be fewer chances of things going wrong when we compose them together into larger complex computations. A good guideline is to try and keep methods around 10 lines of code.

Preventing side effects

This basically means that each small function should not save some state outside itself. Try to limit the use of global variables as much as possible and think of each function as:

1. Data arrives
2. Perform some operation on the data
3. Return results

This way we can easily test each function independently, without worrying about the effect it has on the global state of the program.

An example with viz.js

To see this in practice, let's take a look at the `scripts/viz.js` program as a template for creating testable code for the data-manipulation functions in the visualization. For this example, we will create a set of simple bars that are based on the profit of an arbitrary dataset. We are given the sales and cost in the data; however, we need to determine the profit for the visualization by subtracting the sales from the cost. In this contrived example, we need a few small helper functions, which are as follows:

- A function to take the original dataset and return a new dataset with the profit calculated
- A function to retrieve an array of unique categories to apply to an ordinal scale
- A function to determine the maximum profit value in order to build the upper bound of our input domain

If we create these functions with the best practices outlined earlier and expose them externally, we can test them in isolation and independently.

Let's take a tour of the script to see how it all works together:

```
if (d3.charts === null || typeof(d3.charts) !== 'object')
{ d3.charts = {}; }
```

Here, we will define the namespace for the chart. In this example, our chart can be instantiated with `d3.charts.viz`. If the d3 object with property charts does not exist or if it is not of the type object, create it, using classical functional inheritance to leverage common patterns from a `base` function:

```
d3.charts.viz = function () {
  // Functional inheritance of common areas
  var my = d3.ext.base();
```

A handy function (see `base.js`) to quickly assign getters/setters to the closure following the pattern in Towards Reusable Charts is as follows:

```
// Define getter/setter style accessors..
// defaults assigned
my.accessor('example', true);
```

We use the `svg` variable at this level of scope to maintain state when quickly appending selectors. The `void 0` is a safer way to initialize the variable as undefined:

```
// Data for Global Scope
var svg = void 0,
    chart = void 0;
```

Define the D3 instance functions that will be used throughout the visualization:

```
// Declare D3 functions, also in instance scope
var x = d3.scale.linear(),
    y = d3.scale.ordinal();
```

The following function represents the main interface to the outside world. There is also a set of setup functions commonly seen in D3 visualizations. The SVG container is set up in a way that can easily look for existing SVG containers in the selector and rebind the data. This makes it much easier to redraw when making subsequent calls with new data:

```
my.draw = function(selection) {
  selection.each(function(data) {
    // code in base/scripts.js
    // resuable way of dealing with margins
    svg = my.setupSVG(this);
    chart = my.setupChart(svg);

    // Create the visualization
    my.chart(data);
  });
};

// main method for drawing the viz
my.chart = function(data) {
  var chartData = my.profit(data);

  x.domain([0, my.profitMax(chartData)])
      .range([0,my.w()]);
  y.domain(my.categories(chartData))
      .rangeRoundBands([0, my.h()], 0.2);

  var boxes = chart.selectAll('.box').data(chartData);

  // Enter
  boxes.enter().append('rect')
      .attr('class', 'box')
      .attr('fill', 'steelblue');

  // Update
  boxes.transition().duration(1000)
      .attr('x', 0)
      .attr('y', function(d) { return y(d.category) })
      .attr('width', function(d) {  return x(d.profit) })
```

```
          .attr('height', y.rangeBand())

    // Exit
    boxes.exit().remove();
  };
```

Notice that the `chart` function relies on several helper functions (shown in the following lines of code) to work with the data. It is also written in such a way that we can take advantage of the enter/update/exit pattern:

```
// Example function to create profit.
my.profit = function(data) {
  return data.map(function(d) {
    d.profit = parseFloat(d.sales) - parseFloat(d.cost);
    return d;
  });
};
```

This function is used to create a new data structure that has profit assigned. Note that it takes one data array in as a parameter and returns a newly constructed array with the profit attribute added. This function is now exposed externally with `viz().profit(data)` and can be easily tested. It does not change any of the outside global variables. It is just data in and new data out.

```
my.categories = function(data) {
  return data.map(function(d) {
    return d.category;
  });
};
```

This is the exact same pattern as `my.profit(data)`. We will take the data structure in as input and return a new data structure, that is, an array of all the categories. In the preceding lines of code, you saw that this is leveraged to create the input domain.

```
my.profitMax = function(data) {
  return d3.max(data, function(d) { return d.profit; });
};
```

Once again, a simple function to take data in, compute the max, and return that maximum value. It is very easy to test and verify with `d3.charts.viz().profitMax(data)`.

```
  return my;
};
```

Unit testing

Now that we have a code base written in a testable way, let's automate those tests so that we do not have to perform them manually and can continue to code and refactor with ease.

If you look at the `spec/viz_spec.js` file, you will note some common patterns when unit testing. The following code is written with a JavaScript unit-testing framework called Jasmine and leverages Karma to execute the tests. You can learn more about the Jasmine syntax, assertions, and other features at `http://jasmine.github.io/1.3/introduction.html`.

The bootstrap project has everything you need to start testing quickly.

The first step is to start our Karma test runner with this line of code:

```
node_modules/karma/bin/karma start
```

This runner will watch every edit of the `viz.js` file or the `viz_spec.js` file. If any changes are detected, it will automatically rerun every test suite and provide output on the console. If all the tests pass, then the output will be all green. If something fails, you will receive a red warning message:

```
'use strict';

describe('Visualization: Stacked', function () {
  var viz;

  var data = [
    {"category": "gold",  "cost": "10",  "sales": "60"},
    {"category": "white", "cost": "20",  "sales": "30"},
    {"category": "black", "cost": "100", "sales": "140"}
  ];
```

Create some test data to test your D3 data-manipulation functions. The preceding `describe` syntax defines the test harness you are about to execute:

```
beforeEach(function() {
  viz = d3.charts.viz()
      .height(600)
      .width(900)
      .margin({top: 10, right: 10, bottom: 10, left: 10});
});
```

Before every test run, create a new instance of the D3 visualization with some default setters:

```
it ('sets the profit', function() {
  var profits = viz.profit(data);
  expect(profits.length).toBe(3);
  expect(profits[0].profit).toBe(50)
});
```

This is our first test case! In this test, we asserted that we are getting a new array from our test data, but with an additional profit attribute. Remember that we created the function to have no side effects and to be a small unit of work. We will the fruits of our labor with this easy-to-test method. Just as we did earlier, we will test the list of categories now:

```
it ('returns a list of all categories', function() {
  var categories = viz.categories(data);
  expect(categories.length).toBe(3);
  expect(categories).toEqual([ 'gold', 'white', 'black' ]);
});
```

And calculate the max profit as follows:

```
it ('calculates the profit max', function() {
  var profits = viz.profit(data);
  expect(viz.profitMax(profits)).toEqual(50);
});
```

The following are additional example tests to validate that the height/width, bearing in mind the margins, is working properly from our base.js function:

```
it ('calculates the height of the chart box', function() {
  expect(viz.h()).toBe(580);
  viz.height(700); // change the height
  viz.margin({top: 20, right: 10, bottom: 10, left: 10})
  expect(viz.h()).toBe(670);
});
```

```
it ('calculates the width of the chart box', function() {
  expect(viz.w()).toBe(880);
  viz.height(700); // change the height
  viz.margin({top: 10, right: 10, bottom: 10, left: 20})
  expect(viz.w()).toBe(870);
});
```

As an experiment, try adding new test cases or editing the existing one. Watch the test runner report different results.

Creating resilient visualization code

We want to make sure that our visualization can react to changing data, with minimal effort from the program that calls our code. One way to test different permutations of data and ensure that the visualization reacts accordingly is to randomly create example data, call the visualization code a number of times, and witness the result. These operations are handled in the `factories` directory. Let's take a look at the `viz_factory.js` file as an example:

```
(function() {
    var viz = d3.charts.viz();
```

Create a variable to store our function with getters and setters as closures. In this example, we will use an anonymous function as a wrapper to execute the code. This prevents conflicts with other JavaScript code and ensures that our visualization will work properly in a protected context:

```
var rand = function() {
  return Math.floor((Math.random() * 10) + 1)
};
```

A simple helper function that generates a random number between 1 and 10 is as follows:

```
var data = function() {
  return [1,2,3].map(function(d,i) {
    var cost = rand();
    var sales = rand();

    return {
      category: 'category-'+i,
      cost: cost,
      sales: cost + sales
    };
  });
};
```

Generate a fake dataset based on random numbers:

```
d3.select("#chart").datum(data()).call(viz.draw);
```

Draw the visualization for the first time using these lines of code:

```
var id = setInterval(function() {
  var d = data();
  console.log('data:', d);
  d3.select("#chart").datum(d).call(viz.draw);
```

```
  }, 2000);
  setTimeout(function() {
  clearInterval(id);
  }, 10000);
```

Set a timer for 10 seconds and bind new data to the visualization on iteration. The expected behavior is that the visualization will redraw itself on each call. Notice how simple it is to pass new data to the visualization. It is a simple selector with a new dataset. We have constructed the reusable visualization code in such a way that it knows how to react appropriately.

To see the results in action, simply launch http-server as follows:

node_modules/http-server/bin/http-server

Now, visit http://localhost:8080.

Adding a new test case

What happens if we change the number of datasets in the array? To test this, let's add a new helper function (called set()) to randomly generate a new set of data with a random number of elements between 1 and 10:

```
var set = function() {
  var k = rand();
  var d = [];
  for (var i = 1; i < k; i++) {
    d.push[i];
  };
  return d;
};
```

Modify the data function slightly. We will print to the console to validate that it is working properly:

```
var data = function() {
  var d = set();
  console.log('d', d);
  return d.map(function(d,i) {
    var cost = rand();
    var sales = rand();

    return {
      category: 'category-'+i,
```

```
        cost: cost,
        sales: cost + sales
      };
    });
};
```

Now, if we look at `http://localhost:8080` again, we can see that the visualization is working properly even with a random amount of data.

Summary

In this chapter, we described the techniques to help test your D3 code base and to keep it healthy over the lifespan of your project. We also went step-by-step through a bootstrap project to help you get started with these examples, and we took a look at a methodology for structuring your work.

Our recommendations are based on many years of experience and many projects delivered using D3. We strongly recommend that you follow good software patterns and focus on tests; this will allow you to perfect your craft. Quality is in your hands now. With this, we say goodbye, and thank you for reading!

Index

Thank you for buying
Learning D3.js Mapping

About Packt Publishing

Packt, pronounced 'packed', published its first book, *Mastering phpMyAdmin for Effective MySQL Management*, in April 2004, and subsequently continued to specialize in publishing highly focused books on specific technologies and solutions.

Our books and publications share the experiences of your fellow IT professionals in adapting and customizing today's systems, applications, and frameworks. Our solution-based books give you the knowledge and power to customize the software and technologies you're using to get the job done. Packt books are more specific and less general than the IT books you have seen in the past. Our unique business model allows us to bring you more focused information, giving you more of what you need to know, and less of what you don't.

Packt is a modern yet unique publishing company that focuses on producing quality, cutting-edge books for communities of developers, administrators, and newbies alike. For more information, please visit our website at www.packtpub.com.

About Packt Open Source

In 2010, Packt launched two new brands, Packt Open Source and Packt Enterprise, in order to continue its focus on specialization. This book is part of the Packt Open Source brand, home to books published on software built around open source licenses, and offering information to anybody from advanced developers to budding web designers. The Open Source brand also runs Packt's Open Source Royalty Scheme, by which Packt gives a royalty to each open source project about whose software a book is sold.

Writing for Packt

We welcome all inquiries from people who are interested in authoring. Book proposals should be sent to author@packtpub.com. If your book idea is still at an early stage and you would like to discuss it first before writing a formal book proposal, then please contact us; one of our commissioning editors will get in touch with you.

We're not just looking for published authors; if you have strong technical skills but no writing experience, our experienced editors can help you develop a writing career, or simply get some additional reward for your expertise.

Mastering D3.js

ISBN: 978-1-78328-627-0   Paperback: 352 pages

Bring your data to life by creating and deploying complex data visualizations with D3.js

1. Create custom charts as reusable components to be integrated with existing projects.

2. Design data-driven applications with several charts interacting between them.

3. Create an analytics dashboard to display real-time data using Node and D3 with real world examples.

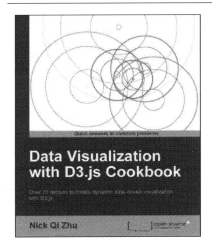

Data Visualization with D3.js Cookbook

ISBN: 978-1-78216-216-2   Paperback: 338 pages

Over 70 recipes to create dynamic data-driven visualization with D3.js

1. Create stunning data visualization with the power of D3.

2. Bootstrap D3 quickly with the help of ready-to-go code samples.

3. Solve real-world visualization problems with the help of practical recipes.

Please check **www.PacktPub.com** for information on our titles

Learning Python Data Visualization

ISBN: 978-1-78355-333-4   Paperback: 212 pages

Master how to build dynamic HTML5-ready SVG charts using Python and the pygal library

1. A practical guide that helps you break into the world of data visualization with Python.

2. Understand the fundamentals of building charts in Python.

3. Packed with easy-to-understand tutorials for developers who are new to Python or charting in Python.

Learning AngularJS [Video]

ISBN: 978-1-78398-506-7   Duration: 02:00 hours

A fast, easy and rewarding way to create web applications with AngularJS

1. Create simple and powerful web applications and learn to make your code reusable.

2. Add resources, directives, services, and factories to increase the efficiency of your app.

3. Get a spectacular and interactive visualization for your app through third-party components such as D3.js, and Bootstrap.

4. Use CSS and animations to make your app look good.

Please check **www.PacktPub.com** for information on our titles

Made in the USA
San Bernardino, CA
05 July 2016